I WENT

TO PRISON

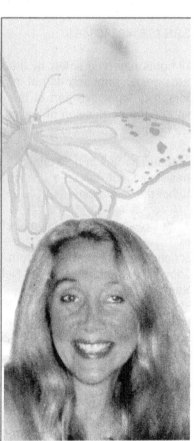

TO BE SET FREE

Susan Folger

EXULON
ELITE

www.xulonpress.com

To
Wilma,

Victory comes
only
in Yeshua! ♥

Susan

11/8/14

To my Trinity God, thank You with my life; I couldn't have written this book if You hadn't changed my heart, but... You did. Father God, You are love and grace! Jesus, You are perfection in demonstrating love and grace! Holy Spirit, You are my power, best friend, teacher/ guide, and writing partner!

I want to thank those that have helped bring this book about. There are many of you that have played a part in this project, even if it was through encouragement. I won't list everyone because I do not want to make any errors and leave someone out. Anyone thinking they had a part in getting this book published, you probably did; you know who you are. Thank you from my heart, I love you!

Table of Contents

WHY WOULD YOU WANT TO READ THIS BOOK OF MY TESTIMONY???

I am not famous—you have never heard of me. I am not splashed across the covers of magazines, or on the nightly news reports. I do not have a well-known popular Christian ministry. **WHO AM I TO YOU** that my story would promote your interest? Why would you spend time reading about someone that you do not even know? Why would my story about meeting the Lord God interest you?

Maybe because I am your family member, your best friend, your next door neighbor, the person sitting next to you in church, the person in line at the grocery store, or in the car next to you in traffic—**MAYBE I AM YOU.**

I am writing this book to share my encounter with the living Lord God, Creator of the universe; how He has completely changed my entire life for good. I want to show others His work in my life, revealing what an awesome God He is.

God is real! God is alive! God is good!

The Lord lives! Blessed be my Rock! Let the God of my salvation be exalted. (Psalm 18:46)

I was a person that did not give much thought at all to God before I met Him in prison. I did not consider Him about anything. I went through life in an emptiness caused by self-indulged thoughts, decisions, and actions. I was so self-absorbed that I could not see beyond my own pain. The daily choices I made from my own attempt to live life put me on a path of destruction. Totally unaware, I was death walking around in a live body.

" In the morning you shall say 'Oh, that it were evening!' And in at evening you shall say 'Oh, that it were morning!'...(Deuteronomy 28:67)

In my own life, I had to be totally free of mind-altering substances before I begin to see the Truth. I took full responsibility for the choices that had escorted me along that wrong path. I repented of a selfish lifestyle that was spiraling downward, and admitted that I had wandered far from where I should be. My choices had placed me in a position where I was humbled beyond the average imagination. I was so far down that I had to look up, "Is there someone higher who cares?"; "Will you help me?". As soon as I did, my Creator God reached down to me.

I desire to share my walk with the living God which will show how He is changing me completely, and effortlessly, as I seek Him daily. He gave me life. He will do this for anyone—He desires to do this for everyone; it is a choice each person has to make for him/herself.

> *"...I have set before you life and death, blessing and cursing, therefore* **choose life** *that both you and your descendants may live...(Deuteronomy 30:19)*

I pray that my experiences with Him will inspire and encourage those reading. I share my day-to-day walk with Him, as He works supernaturally in my life, revealing things to me that were always there; I just could not see them—He opened my eyes.

There is a new and wonderful life for anyone who will accept Him. It does not matter the individual circumstances—what you've done, your age, your income, your past beliefs; nothing matters from your past if you give your future to the living Lord Jesus Christ.

> *...he who has seen has testified, and his testimony is true; and he knows that he is telling the truth, so that you may believe. (John 19:35)*

CHAPTER 1

THE PUZZLE PIECES DO NOT FIT

*B*y looking at my outward appearance, I don't believe most people suspected that inside I was a completely fragmented person. It might have appeared that I had it all together.

I came across fairly polished in my disguise to a world that did not know my inner turmoil. I am not talking about those who knew me intimately—they knew I had issues. Even to those knowing me as an acquaintance, there were evident signs that my life was less than blessed, but…to the world that saw me in public, I seemed to possess a life that might have been envied.

The truth was that I wearing a mask to conceal the pain of a very dysfunctional life. I had put this mask on at a very young age, and I had learned to wear it well. I kept it polished, keeping it pretty and fixed perfectly in place, so that it would hide the cracks.

My family life was one of alcoholic dysfunction. Both my parents suffered from the effects of alcohol that constantly ravaged their lives. My mom also took prescription drugs, or I should say she abused prescription drugs. The thing is, the consequences of their addictions were not unique to them, but spilled out into the lives of everyone around. That would include me and my sister Sylvia (six years older), and my Granny Lou (adopted my mom as a baby) who spent a lot of weekdays at our house trying to help (caring for the family; household chores, etc.).

An overdose of prescription drugs and alcohol ultimately caused the death of my mom at the age of 45. Her death caught me by surprise. We had talked two days before on the phone, and in an inebriated state she told me she would see me before long. Well, I did see her soon, but it was in a coffin.

I was told she died of heart failure. Around 5 years later I saw her death certificate; it stated heart failure resulting from an overdose of drugs and alcohol. My dad had attempted to cover the details of her death. Sadness enveloped me over the loss of my mother, who I had seen captured by a state of addiction, and over the feeble attempts of my dad to perpetuate the lie of addiction that had always been denied in my family.

My dad drank a lot after the death of my mom, and continued to do so until he was diagnosed with cancer. He died 3 years after my mom; he was 57. I felt a kind of relief at the passing of my dad because toward the end he looked to be in his eighties. He had suffered 2 years fighting this disease, and it had taken its toll.

I experienced some pretty harsh things as a child growing up. I will share only a few instances because the day to day harsh realities of alcoholic dysfunction would take up volumes. Things that happened at home stayed behind the walls of our house. This was the model I used to practice the art of wearing my personal mask. You do not let the outside world know that things are less that perfect, or so I had been taught through personal observation of my parents.

"How are you, Susan?" I would smile, and say "I'm just fine". This automatic response of gesture and words was an attempt to hide the complete inadequacy I felt inside.

My dad, Walter Jones, was well-liked, intelligent, and successful in business. He owned a small company, and in addition acquired several pieces of real estate. He achieved a level of income that would allow for many physical comforts. He was able to accomplish these things in the midst of his drinking.

My mom, Peggy, was also intelligent and likeable. Even though she stayed at home most of my life, in her early thirties she trained to be a radiological technologist, and then worked at Harris hospital in Ft. Worth Texas for a couple of years.

Alcoholism, or any addictive lifestyle, does not necessarily fit into the stereotype of that person. Addiction is certainly not limited to the "skid row" perception that some people have. Bottom line is that addictions are not selective as they cross all borders of socio-economic, cultural, educational, and intelligence levels. The majority of people nurse their addictions behind closed doors of "normalcy".

To the outside world, my family would have the appearance of being successful and happy (I would later find out at a family reunion that extended family members were fooled also). Success is quite often the image projected by people desperately trying to convey the "good life" while in reality they are suffering every day in immense inner pain and turmoil.

From my very early years as a toddler I sensed that my family was not normal. Today as I write my story, I realize that my upbringing is quite typical. Maybe the details are different, but the essence is the same. I could not see then that a lot of families were dysfunctional; they wore disguises also. I thought my family was unique, and I was ashamed of what went on behind closed doors.

Loud and ugly verbal fights between my parents were not uncommon. Sometimes these would be accompanied by holes being punched in a wall or door, or the breaking of an item. I can remember my mom throwing an entire cake into the floor in a fit of rage. "Hadn't mommy made that cake for us?"

When these incidents occurred they were inexpressibly scary. I would try and escape this loud and live nightmare by hiding under my bed, or inside my closet. **I was seeking peace in dark, closed-in places.** If I was already in bed when the screaming started, I would pull the covers over my head; I wondered if I could be part of the cause of the fighting. **Maybe if I hid nobody would see me.**

16

To this day, I find it comfortable to snuggle in the womb of my bed; early childhood memories (both good and bad) are very powerful and long-lasting.

My dad traveled weekdays during my early childhood. The weekend party started when he got home on Friday. Football was a big event on Saturday and Sunday afternoons, and of course these occasions involved drinking a lot of beer and whiskey. My dad would yell at the players to such a degree that I associated cussing with the game; consequently, I never enjoyed football.

The weekend mornings allowed no noise that would complicate the hangovers. This did not leave much room for kids to be kids. I didn't want to make any noise that might cause my mom and dad to get mad and yell at me. **Maybe if I was quiet nobody would hear me.**

My sister and I were home with our mother during those weekdays when our dad traveled. She often coped with her responsibilities in the way that she was comfortable with—drinking and drugs. It was not abnormal for my mom to stumble around the house in an intoxicated state. There were also times when my mom drove inebriated. This endangered not only her life, but our lives, and the lives of others.

There were two separate occurrences when my dad and my mother each wrecked a car with me and my sister inside. My dad was driving our family home from an adult party one night; my mom was passed out in the back seat, and Sylvia and I were in the front. A pole got in the way of the front of our car, and my dad hit it head-on. I can remember the dash lights and headlights still being on, and illuminating my dad as his head was slumped on the steering wheel. Sylvia and I had no option but to sit in the wrecked car and wait until our dad woke up and drove us home.

My mom was attempting to drive Sylvia and me someplace in the daytime, but a ditch got in the way; the car stopped just a few feet short of entering a pond. Because we were on the private road to our house, Sylvia and I were able to get out of the car and walk home. My mother's head was resting on the steering wheel just as our dad's had been.

Fortunately, both of these incidents happened in the country, and no other car was involved. My sister and I were not hurt physically, but even though there were no physical wounds, intense emotional wounds were inflicted and ran deep. These wrecks occurred when I was pre-kindergarten age, but mental images of my passed-out parents behind the wheel of the car are still vivid.

These times were not discussed at all, never mentioned. **Maybe if we didn't talk about these horrors, they didn't happen**, but.... they did. In an attempt to make things normal, these episodes were swept under the rug, but they were hiding in our hearts and minds to manifest one day in their own bizarre behavior.

My family lived in the country 30 miles south of the Ft. Worth/ Dallas metro-plex. There were no neighborhood kids to play with after school, or during the summer. This was a relief, in a way, because I was terrified someone would find out what went on inside my house. Even until the day I left for college, at the age of seventeen, I had anxiety about friends coming over.

There was no consistency of behavior, and no guarantee of a welcoming environment to my guests. I was humiliated innumerable times in front of friends as one, or both, of my parents made an uninvited drunken appearance during a visit.

The nature around me became a source of comfort as I took refuge in long walks through acres of cotton, or pasture fields full of flowers. This source of life (which I always believed God created) gave me respite from the dead environment inside the house where I grew up. I had learned by necessity to spend time by myself, but I very much wanted to be a part of something, and somebody.

The guilt and shame of the dysfunction I was experiencing gave me the message that I did not fit in anywhere. **Maybe if I would try hard enough, nobody would know my pain and discomfort—** maybe there was a place for me.

I quietly excelled in school (National Honor Society), wore nice clothes, and had impeccable manners. **Maybe I could blend in and nobody would know I was different. Maybe if I could be smart enough, or nice enough, or pretty enough.....**

Even amidst this chaotic life, I knew my parents and my sister loved me. I also loved both my parents and my sister. Our parents provided for us in physical ways, and gave as much emotionally as they were able. There was never a lack of things money could buy including education and culture. My parents would later pay for me to attend many years of college.

Those attempts of a normal loving atmosphere could not make up for the incomplete, and inconsistent, emotional availability that was the stark reality.

Because of family life being a mixture of normalcy amidst insane chaos, my own life was developing into a state of complexity. There was a longing to be noticed and to be somebody important, but this was in direct conflict with my desire to just fade into the background. I was one confused and lost little girl.

CHAPTER 2

LOOKING FOR
THE MISSING "PEACE"

*A*s I grew older, I discovered there was a variety of ways to disguise the hurt and fear ingrained in me at a young age. I was a teenager in the sixties, and sex, drugs, and rock and roll were coming into mainstream America. These things appealed to me, in a sort of rebellious way, as the means to cope with issues of life. Drugs would begin to play a very dominate part in my life over the next 4 decades. Attempts to numb myself from the hurts of the world by using mind-altering substances (seeking peace in dark, closed-in places) would eventually make mediocrity my accepted life-style.

I began smoking marijuana at the age of fifteen. **Maybe if I just got high I wouldn't have to feel any pain in life.** It was also at that very young age that I lost my precious virginity—something I could never recover. I gave the purity of my body to an older surfer boy

I met while on family vacation at the beach. I was trying to be all grown up in a cool and popular way. I wanted to be someone special to a boy I would never see again. I believe this very foolish and permanent decision was a direct result of my smoking marijuana that day. The mood alteration of the drug allowed me to cast my inhibitions and good judgment to the wind.

I embellished the effects of marijuana with alcohol as often as I could get hold of it. It was not difficult for me to secure marijuana or alcohol. I did not have to buy these substances because there are always boys who want to share drugs and get high with a pretty, and willing, girl. Maybe there will be something in it for them?? There seemed to be a sense of control in this newly found power (drugs and boys) over my life. This gave me a very counterfeit feeling of acceptance (fitting in), and love. It was amazing how often opportunities manifested to put these drugs into my life, but... **it was me who always made the ultimate decision to use them.**

In the beginning marijuana and alcohol appeared to work pretty good for me. For the first time I seemed to fit in. I felt calm, cool, and proud to be part of a growing, but still sub-culture crowd. I thought these substances were the answer to my problems. I did not give much thought to the fact that marijuana was illegal, or to the fact that I was underage to be drinking alcohol.

Amazingly, I did not really give much weight to the fact that alcohol had caused such devastating and painful things in my life growing up. I was <u>deceived</u> in my thinking that alcohol and drugs were not harmful to me because I was maintaining my high grades in school. I was <u>deceived</u> in my thinking that I was handling things in life...unlike my parents. I was self-satisfied in the fact that I was able to hide their usage from those in authority. I can remember going places and being smug that I was high, and people around me did not know. My parents were even fooled for quite a while.

Even though my parents had issues with alcohol, or maybe because they did, they did not want to see me go down the same road they were traveling. More than once they talked to me about alcohol—especially in my early twenties during my first divorce. They sat me down, and told me that additional problems would manifest in my life because of alcohol, "Susan, you need to watch your drinking, or it will get you into trouble". They even told me that my Granny Lou was very disappointed in my usage of alcohol. I never wanted to hurt the granny I loved so very much; the one who had provided major emotional stability in my life.

The love for another person will not usually stop the insanity of using drugs/alcohol, or any addictive behavior, for very long. I witnessed the hurt and destruction that my drug/alcohol usage caused those I loved. Hurting others always made me ashamed, and gave me a resolve to stop, and I absolutely meant it.....until next time.

I did not listen to what my parents told me in my early twenties. How could they advise me when they were still actively drinking? Their speaking to me came from a wisdom and knowledge that was obtained from experience, but I didn't hear what they were trying

23

to tell me. I needed to hear personal events in their life leading up to the usage of alcohol, and how it had subsequently affected them.

I believe if they had shared specific, and personal, details of their battle with alcohol, I might have been more apt to listen. Instead, they focused on why I shouldn't drink—in a preachy sort of way. Their focus on my not drinking alcohol seemed to make me even more determined to use it (rebellion). I had convinced myself that what I was doing was all right—I was in complete control.

It is a powerful thing when someone shares from their own experiences. There is a realness that comes across to another person. An attempt to help someone through accusation, judgment, and criticism is usually rejected, but sharing our own downfalls from a sincere heart of love imparts a positive impact of healing.

I regularly used the drugs of alcohol and marijuana during my last two years of high school, and continued to use them in college. I used them to enjoy a good day, and I used them to harbor me through a rough day. The thing is that in college, I began using many other drugs as well. I wanted to go further in my quest for "the fabulous life".

There were not many drugs that I did not use, or many ways to ingest them that I did not try. I regularly used cocaine, barbiturates, opiates, amphetamines, many types of psychedelic drugs, and various others. I also used heroin a few times. I was <u>deceived</u> in my thinking that because I had never put a needle into my arm to use intravenously, I had a firm grip on the usage of these drugs.

As the years passed, the fact that I had over 6 years of college, but no degree, should have given an indication to the reality that there was a problem. I was <u>deceived,</u> and complacent, with the fact that I had maintained high grades (dean's list), but had just not found my true calling.

I was in my mid-twenties when my mother and father passed. I was left a very generous inheritance (which should have lasted throughout my natural life). I decided that I would live on the interest until I figured out my exact vocation. I did work at a few jobs like waitressing, and for some years in large health clubs as a nationally certified aerobic-dance instructor. These jobs did not reflect the level of education that I had achieved, but they gave me flexibility of schedule to fit my leisurely life-style, which included "out in the open" (with others) drug and alcohol adventures.

My waitress jobs were definitely influenced by drugs and alcohol. Many "employee meetings" were held during shifts (these would entail drinking "shots" of hard liquor), and many tips included lines of cocaine, as well as money.

I was also high on something every time I taught an aerobics class. I thought I danced better when I was high. Think of the insanity of being high while promoting fitness. Because I was able to maintain these jobs, I was <u>deceived</u> in my thinking that I was in control.

I had married after my first year of college (at eighteen), but divorced around the age of twenty-one. I married another man at the age of twenty-nine, after living together for 6 years. This marriage also ended in divorce after 10 years. In both marriages, the regular use of some form of drugs and alcohol continued as a part of our lives.

The man I married at eighteen was my high school sweetheart. I was fifteen when I met Jerry in the parking lot of a hamburger stand in the neighboring town where he lived. I was immediately drawn to his long hair. He struck me as sort of defiant in the way he drove around in his 1955 Chevy hot-rod. I liked the fact that this older guy had his own car. When we smoked pot on our first date, the romance was sealed.

I met my second husband in the bar where I worked at the time. Tris was tall and handsome. When he picked me up for our first rendezvous, he had his dog, Karma, with him. That closeness with his dog was very impressive to me. When we snorted cocaine, the romance was sealed. In fact, he moved into my house that very night.

I truly loved (and liked) both of these men; I am in contact with them to this day. Drugs were the initial sealing bond to each relationship, and played too big a part in our lives. Because of this, the marriages were destined to fail. The very thing that drew me to them (our mutual hedonistic attitudes) should have been a huge alert.

Don't misunderstand. There were many great times and good memories with these men. It is just amazing that I never gave any thought to what I might want in a marriage; no expectations of the man that was to be my husband. In both marriages, we lived self-ishly for the moment without giving consideration to each other, or to our future together. Drugs and alcohol were a huge intrusion to our lives, marring the image of the lovely picture that could have developed without them.

Drugs and alcohol were what we did in social situations ("fun"?), and what we did daily as a way to smooth out the harsh realities of a world that can be unpleasant. Do a majority of people go through daily life this same way? Yes. Is this the best way? No!

It is incredible how my lifestyle reflected that of my parents. There was a difference in detail, but the exact same vain attempt of misery seeking to find peace and acceptance through mood-altering substances and experiences.

Over the years, from my teenage days into my fifties, I searched for answers to bring peace in my life. It began with drug experimentation, and progressed to attendance of psychic fairs, and new-age events. I saw no harm in dabbling in tarot card and palm readings, or attending séances. It seemed harmless (almost fun) to get direction from the spiritual world (which I did not really perceive as genuine). I absolutely did not understand the reality of spiritual beings (both Divine and demonic). These spiritual forces I played around with were from the demonic realm, and they were out to do me harm.

I read many new-age books, and listened to countless new-age teachings. I was seeking; I perceived these to be a positive way to live. "**I** could do it", "**I** had the power to change".

27

" In the pride of your heart you say, "I am a god..."...

but you are a man and not a god, though you think

you are as wise as a god. (Ezekiel 28:2, NIV)*

None of these things availed any change in my life except to open myself up to a real, and very dark, demonic spiritual dimension that I did not intend to enter. The devil and his demons are subtly deceiving people at all times, and they are viciously wicked.

"...this is your hour—when darkness reigns."

(Luke 22:53, NIV)*

During my second marriage, we lived in another country (Costa Rica) for a few years. We had gone there on vacation, and because it was very beautiful and tranquil, we decided to experience living in the tropics for a while. It was there that I began using a highly addictive anti-anxiety medication.

Can you imagine that my life in that tropical paradise was so "stressful" that I had to resort to using valium daily to calm myself? Even living amidst this serene environment I was anxious and insecure inside, and thought the valium would help bring needed peace to my life. I bought and used this medication in secret, and I perceived my new addiction to be unnoticed by others. In reality, changes the medication brought to my personality were obvious to all.

When we moved back to the states, I located doctors that would prescribe a similar medication (xanax) to valium. I thought I could not function without it. I was addicted to it both physically and emotionally, but was in complete denial to this fact. I couldn't see the problem in taking xanax daily to cope with life. I had virtually stopped using illegal drugs, but now I was <u>deceived</u> by the lie that because this new "high" was prescribed, I was complying with society and its laws. "There is no problem; this medication is legally prescribed by a doctor." "I need these pills; they are helping me!"

The day came when my past behaviors caught up to me. I had been using illegal drugs, and driving intoxicated for decades, but under the <u>deceit</u> that it was ok because "I am not hurting anyone else". Up to this point I had escaped any legal consequences.

> *Do not be deceived: God cannot be mocked. A man reaps what he sows. The one who sows to please his sinful nature, from that nature will reap destruction... (Galatians 6:7-8, NIV)*

Legal issues (arrests) began to appear in my life at a steady rate—all alcohol-related incidents; I was also taking the xanax. By itself this anti-anxiety medication can be dangerous, but mixed with alcohol it made a deadly cocktail. Drugs and alcohol are common ways to relax, and I convinced myself they would someday, somehow, work for me. After all, a majority of people in our society use them…don't they?

The first arrest (January 1995) occurred one night after spending a few hours with friends, drinking wine and dancing (partying and unwinding) at a nightclub. I left there feeling really good, and ready to tackle whatever the next day would bring. On the way home I drove past a local, well-known (by me) police station at twenty miles per hour over the speed limit; I was insanely tempting fate. Of course my intoxication was obvious to the officer who pulled me over for speeding, and I was given a breath-test (which I failed). I was arrested for DWI (driving while intoxicated), taken inside that police station, and placed in a cell where I remained overnight; I was literally (physically throwing up), and emotionally (deep sadness) sick.

I was horrified and ashamed that I had been arrested. How could a well-educated and cultured woman like me go to jail? How had my life come to this? It had been slowly happening all along, but I had denied the overwhelming facts that pointed to the coming destruction. The very next day I began to attend Alcoholics Anonymous regularly.

I knew there was a problem, but I still refused to look at the real issue…Me. I wasn't really ready to give up the alcohol and drugs that were "aiding" this insanity. This lifestyle was complete madness, and yet, in a very strange way I was comfortable with it because it patterned the environment in which I grew up.

In less than 2 years I was arrested numerous times, and the day came that I was convicted of a felony for intoxicated assault. This felony arrest happened on the way home after a night in jail for a second DWI. No, I never even made it home! I was taken right back to the same jail. I was in my forties.

The second DWI occurred after an afternoon in a restaurant-bar (October 1996); I had just finished probation (two weeks earlier) for the first DWI. I truly do not remember what "trauma" happened to convince me I should go out and drink, but apparently something occurred that I thought alcohol and pills would fix. They fixed it all right—all the way to jail.

The next afternoon, I was driven to my impounded car by the husband of a woman that I met in jail. Immediately, I took several xanax that I had in the car, and then I had the "insane" idea to go to a restaurant for dinner and wine. "I was tired and hungry after having spent 24 hours in jail". On the way home from the restaurant, I smashed into the back of a car that was stopped at a red light. This would turn out to be a felony DWI intoxicated assault. I wouldn't get my fourth DWI until 12 years later.

My truck was totaled, but I didn't seem to give much concern to the fact that this was the fourth car (yes, 4) in under 2 years that I demolished. "Insurance will handle it!" Somehow these wrecks seemed mundane to me (just a day in the life of an addict).

In two of these wrecks, I ran off the road after leaving bars (needless to say, drunk), and the cars rolled over into destruction.

These occurrences took place in the country; fortunately, no other car was involved (remember the wrecks of my parents?). The other wreck involved my car, as one of six, in a pile-up that had already occurred on the interstate. I was drinking a wine cooler when I added to the line of 5 cars; otherwise I might have been able to stop in time. In each wreck, I had my cars towed by a wrecker, and got a ride home. I put my money to use, and proceeded to buy another car after each incident.

Even as I write this today **I am shocked by my thinking process, making the same choices to drink and do drugs over and over, amidst adverse results that proved to be intensifying each time they were recreated.** It is absolutely astounding that I didn't kill, or permanently maim myself...I wasn't even physically injured in any of the wrecks.

The day of the third DWI intoxicated assault I was so messed up by those xanax pills, I did not realize the gravity of the fact that when I hit the car from behind, 2 kids had been injured. I was so numbed by that medication that I was focused more on the legal repercussions for my life than on the fact that I had injured kids, and that the incident could have killed somebody.

"I'm scared, will I go to jail for this?" "This is going to cost me a lot of money in attorney fees, but maybe they can get me out of this mess." "I'm embarrassed, what will people think when they hear I've been arrested again?" Me, me, me....oh, my, my, my!

"...He feels but the pain of his own body and mourns only for himself ." (Job 14:22, NIV)

I was frustrated that I had been caught and arrested. I thought the laws were unfair and harsh. I was deeply ashamed on some inner level, and yet, DWIs are so common these days in our society that I convinced myself the wreck was an irritating and unfortunate accident that just compounded the DWI arrest. I soothed myself by using those substances in greater quantities. This was an attempt to try and cover up the reality that my life was out of control, and that it might be my fault through bad choices.

Even though we were divorced, I lived with my second husband, Tris, during those arrests in my forties. Eventually I bought another house, moved out, and lived on my own. I was trying desperately to do the right things. One day I fell on my deck and broke my femur. Do I have to state that I had been drinking? Don't forget that I was taking anti-anxiety medication. This incident prompted the taking of narcotic pain medications (vicodin/hydrocodone). After some time the surgeon would not prescribe more, so I proceeded to find another way to obtain them — legally, of course!

It is not difficult to obtain prescriptions for powerful narcotic drugs these days. I was absolutely convinced that I was in severe pain every month when I went into the pain clinic to get my prescription from those "legal drug dealers".

Now I was addicted to alcohol, anti-anxiety medication (xanax), and narcotic drugs (vicodin/hydrocodone); I was <u>deceived</u> in my thinking that this was ok because these drugs were legal. I did not drive while drinking anymore; however, it never entered my mind that every time I drove I was breaking a law because I was driving under the influence of strong, mind-altering prescription drugs.

The law makes no qualifying distinction about what makes a person impaired. If someone is driving under the influence of alcohol, or any type of medication that affects the ability of driving, then they are breaking the law. It is not worth the risk to the one driving, or to the innocent person that might be in their pathway. Again, I have to reflect back on the parallel of my life to that of my parents; it was astounding!

The fact is that these medications were very toxic to my life. I truly did not think I could live without those pills. I was <u>deceived</u> in my thinking it a huge plus that people did not see me take these pills, nor was there any smell on my breath from them—unlike alcohol. I did not drink daily, but I thought I needed those pills every single day to survive. I could not imagine living without the perceived "security" they gave me.

I never considered that others saw me differently than I saw myself. I had taken those medications so long that I thought I was functioning normally. Deep down I knew that I was addicted, but I thought I was handling things—can you believe it? Later, after coming home from prison, people that had not known me before I started taking those medications told me they had thought I was "a dingy blond" or "mentally challenged"—oh, my goodness!

The usage of them became totally insane. I thought I could not function without them. I took a little pill to get up in the morning. I took a little pill to go to sleep at night. I took many little pills in between morning and night. I took a little pill to make a phone-call. I even took a little pill to walk my dog, or to take a shower.

There were so many real demonic spiritual forces at work in my life that I was under a concentrated attack in my own home. I was bound up in a tightly woven demonic spiritual snare of bondage that was initiated by, but exceeded, the drug usage. My lifestyle over the decades had literally invited demonic spiritual forces into my life. These demonic forces were always with me, but there was an intense, tangible awareness of them inside my home; this consciousness appeared to be more acute when I was alone (without the distracting interference of people, music, or tv). It got so bad that it was difficult for me to leave my house; I was in the clutches of perceptible demonic influence. When I did manage to get dressed and drive away, the relief I felt was immediate upon driving out my driveway, but demonic spiritual heaviness was waiting for me on my return.

...we do not wrestle against flesh and blood, but against powers, against the rulers of the darkness of this age, against spiritual hosts of wickedness...

(Ephesians 6:12)

I was in trouble, but I was <u>deceived</u> by the lie that I had to have those pills for survival in life. My life was not my own anymore. I had become a slave to the dark forces of evil. I was physically alive, and walking around in the flesh, but I was completely dead on the inside.

My life was about to change. I was about to experience a life without those little pills, without alcohol, without any artificial method of survival. I was about to live life without the lies that had brought me misery all of my life. I was about to meet my Maker who would introduce me to myself.

I was about to get rid of the <u>deceit,</u> and meet the Truth. Jesus said, *"...I am..Truth..." John 14:6.*

I was about to be set free.

...you shall know the truth, and the truth shall make you free. (John 8:32)

CHAPTER 3

I WAS BOUND

I went to prison to be set free. It certainly did not start out that way. When I got my fourth DWI (driving while intoxicated) on 8/8/8, I thought my life was over. I now know the number eight means "A New Beginning". During the 11 months of fighting the DWI charge, it seemed like anything but that.

I don't remember all details of the morning on 8/8/8, but like the first 3 DWIs, deception made me think drugs and alcohol would soothe the situation. I went to a restaurant for lunch, and ordered a margarita. For some reason I did not drink it, but got up and left. Apparently I had taken too many vicodin and xanax pills that morning, and the wait- person sensed something was terribly wrong with me. Later, I found out they called the police. I didn't make it very far from the restaurant before I saw a police car coming toward me. When it turned around and started following my car, I knew it wasn't long before I would be pulled over.

I had pills with me, and immediately took several by chewing them up. I wanted to calm myself, and I also did not want the police to find them. When I was given the breath-test, it showed no alcohol, but I was obviously high. Because I already had a felony for the intoxicated assault, a judge was contacted, and he ordered a blood test which would reveal prescription drugs. I was taken to jail, and placed into a holding cell.

I spent a couple nights in jail before my bond was placed at $50,000. This would be the start of a 9 month tour before a judge. I had to appear personally each month (couldn't be represented by an attorney because of my past felony). I seriously contemplated ending my life during those months. I was so very tired, confused, and defeated. My life was totally chaotic…I felt completely hopeless!

This was not the first time I had considered suicide. I made several attempts to end my life throughout my 54 years. In my early twenties a pill overdose landed me in the hospital for an all night stay to have my stomach pumped. One of my later attempts (in my forties, but before the arrests began), to cut my wrists, landed me in a psychiatric ward for an overnight evaluation; I put on my favorite mask, and cleverly convinced the doctor I was "just fine". Both of these attempts were fueled by drugs and alcohol.

I was feeling desperation of inner pain that I thought could only be removed by taking my life. It didn't seem like I was contributing anything to this world. I felt like a loser who wouldn't be missed (drugs and alcohol only reinforced this thinking). These attempts to end my life were in actuality loud screams from a deep desire to live.

I can look back and see how very selfish this thinking was (just like all of my wrong thinking was "**self**"ish). I wasn't thinking of how family members and friends would be directly affected by my suicide. On some inner level, I had bought into the lie that there was nobody outside of self that really cared about me. I was very wrong; Jesus loves me (always has, always will), and suicide would have been eternally tragic!

The reality was that I never considered I might be a part of something larger than what my human eyes could see—that I had been made by the Creator God (He makes no junk!), and that He had plans for my life.

> *...**I know the thoughts I think toward you, says the Lord**, thoughts of peace and not evil, to give you a future and a hope. Then you will **call upon Me** and go and **pray to Me** and **I will listen to you** and you will **seek Me** and find Me when you **search for Me** with all your heart. I will be found by you says the Lord, and **I will bring you back from your captivity**... (Jeremiah 29:11-14)*

Each month (2008 and 2009) when I entered into the courtroom and stood in front of a Williamson County judge I became more hopeless and suicidal. Our God already had plans for me to enter into a Williamson County courtroom (again) each month, beginning in 2014, to pray for our country with a judge and a few other women. Wow, yes, that has happened, but back then I could never have been convinced that it would. I couldn't have imagined what good my future held, but my God knew, and He knew how to accomplish it.

This truth of how God loves His creations is found in the Bible. I had never taken the time to read it. Instead, I had fooled around with alcohol, drugs, and false teachings that took me nowhere except the darkness of bondage.

On July 29, 2009, I was sentenced to 5 years prison in Texas Department of Criminal Justice (TDCJ). The day before that sentencing, I sat in my attorney's office and said to a friend that even though I had always believed God created the beautiful universe, I did not believe that Jesus Christ was the Son of God. I was speaking out of ignorance. I did not know anything the Bible taught about our God. Going to church as a kid, and again a few years prior to my fourth DWI arrest, taught me very little about our Creator-God, and absolutely nothing about how to be in relationship with Him.

I had heard about You [only] by the hearing of the ear… (Job 42:5, AMP)

My mother had seen to it that Sylvia and I went to Sunday School and church regularly. Most often we were dropped off and picked up. My parents were trying to introduce us to God, but His personal realness comes only from the reality of having an intimate relationship with Him. My parents did not have this relationship with Him. Instead, these unpleasant church experiences were outward attempts at knowing God. These excursions actually made things worse.

As a child, I did not feel special attention or love from those leaders at the church. I did not see that much difference from what I saw at home—mixed behavior that often differed from words spoken. It got to where I dreaded church, and the day came, at around the age of twelve, that I quit going. Maybe God did not care about me either. I would not waste my time thinking about a God who I believed created the universe, but was remote from the humans on earth.

The day of my sentencing turned out to be the first day that I would begin to realize what a very real, very alive, and very awesome Lord we have. His name is Jesus Christ. He began introducing Himself to me in a very personal way.

...now my [spiritual] eye sees You. (Job 42:5, AMP)

Our God desires to be a personal Lord to each of His creations. He knows all intricacies of each person; this is because He created them. This world causes distortion of the person our God intended, but He is well able to work through that, and restore His intention. He knows exactly how to speak with each person so that they will understand it is Him who is talking. God wants to communicate one on one, but.....you have to seek Him.

Our God is a gentleman; He will not violate the free will that He gave each of us. If a person doesn't want God in their life, He will not force them.

The realization that I was going to prison placed me in a state of shock. Five years in prison seemed an eternity, but in reality I had been imprisoned for decades. For 40 years, drugs, alcohol, and sex had been my method of coping with the bound-up and very confused identity of the true me. The substance abuse and sex were only symptoms of the underlying issue, ME....**I did not know who I was**. I was in bondage to insecurity, self-doubt, and fear. I had been running from myself for 40 years, but...everywhere I went there I was! I was lost and very miserable, and had been since before my teen years.

I was beginning the journey to a final destination that would give me the peace and acceptance I had sought through superficial means. Those things never worked for me, and will never work for anyone. I was learning that brief excitement of external pleasure will eventually be overshadowed by an unbearable darkness. I had been groping under a veil of bleak obscurity, in desperation of Light that can only be found in Jesus Christ.

I was totally exhausted. It is hard work to live life that involves going against the norm of laws enforced by our society. The core of these laws (Ten Commandments) is clearly outlined in the Bible. The eternal principle of these laws (love), spoken out of the heart of our Creator God, is spiritually, morally, and civilly perfect…**yes, even in this twenty-first century**.

The timeless execution of these laws is **LOVE**. If I had acted out of the love expected by our Creator, none of these commandments would have been broken. I couldn't have truly walked in love, and blatantly dishonored any of them. That kind of love proved to be too hard for me! Instead, I followed my own self-willed passion in a defiance which caused me to ignore this divine love principle.

…love is the fulfillment of the law.(Romans 13:10)

I broke every one of God's Ten Commandments during my 40 years of selfish rebellion against God's blessings. Yes… all ten!

1. You must not have any gods before the Living God (our Creator God had very little place in my life—He was pretty much non-existent to me).

2. You must not make for yourself an idol (drugs, alcohol, people, my dogs, etc. were more important to me than God).

3. You must not misuse the name of God (my lifestyle was constantly disrespectful to His name, which represents all integrity).

4. Remember to observe the Sabbath (most of my life I didn't even give thought of this as a holy day of rest).

5. Honor your father and mother (I often did not give respect to them).

6. You must not murder (I killed life in my own body two times through abortion).

7. You must not commit adultery (in each of my marriages).

8. You must not steal (I shoplifted many times).

9. You must not lie against your neighbor (I did not hesitate if it fit my agenda).

10. You must not covet your neighbor's property (not only literal possessions, but even things like someone's boyfriend/husband, popularity, or intellect).

Of course I did not see it that way. **I thought I was a pretty good person**, attempting to stay within the general perimeter of societal laws. By not complying with human laws (like stealing), and sometimes in direct compliance with legal ruling such as with abortion, I inadvertently ignored the divine laws of the universe set up by our Creator God. I believe all acts of sin originate from breaking one of the Ten Commandments.

Human beings have an innate way of cleverly disguising their sin; they are convinced that everything is fine. It is amazing how the human mind and heart work together to format the capacity of deception.

> *The heart is deceitful above all things, and desperately wicked…..(Jeremiah 17:9)*

During the three months leading up to the sentencing, I voluntarily entered an in-patient drug rehabilitation center. If the sentence turned out to be prison, I was not going in addicted to drugs, where there would be no mercy on my condition. The withdrawal would be potentially dangerous (shocking to my system), very rough; I wanted help.

The particular rehab I chose is based on solid, spiritual, Biblical principles from the Alcoholics Anonymous 12-step program (which has aided the recovery of many people). After spending an uncomfortable week to detoxify (ridding my body of the poisonous drugs, under medical supervision), I began going through the 12 steps, and taking a very truthful and depth-probing look inside.

The fourth step had me write down major unpleasant things (resentments) done in my life (by me and others). The fifth step was telling someone else these things I had written; this brought my past dark deeds out into the open light. The ninth step was to make direct amends to people I had hurt. I physically dealt with the people I could, but to those not still living, or to those that would have been hurt by past deeds they were unaware of, I wrote letters of apology; then I tore up those letters.

To be honest, I began doing these steps because it was required in this rehab, and I also thought it would look good to the court-system. The fact is, that in doing these steps, I saw in my heart that I had not been a very nice person; I was saddened by my past behavior. Being honest about my part of life's "tragedies", being remorseful for them, and really wanting to change, turned out to be the heartfelt repentance I would need to enter the eternal kingdom of God. Repentance is simply (1) being humble, (2) taking personal responsibility for past actions, and (3) having sincere willingness to alter these wrongs, and go another direction in life.

The necessary job of digging deep was not particularly pleasant. I had never done it completely sober, or from a sincere heart. For the first time, I did not just go through the steps with superficial lip-service. I looked at my life, and took full responsibility for the decisions and actions made. It didn't matter what someone had done to me; it didn't matter what someone had not done for me.

I was dismayed by my part; the bottom line proved it was me who made the choices affecting my life's destiny. Nobody made me choose the path I had taken. I had deliberately taken the route that brought me to destruction. My own willful thinking had been the problem!

...the root of the matter is found in me (Job 19:28)

Yes, I had a rough childhood, but I also had a good mind with which to think through and make solid decisions about my life. I had willfully bought into lies that I thought gave me an easy way out of problems here on earth. Those "in the moment", unwise choices, created overwhelming future problems. I would never have imagined I would be in a rehab getting off prescription drugs due to the looming threat of prison.

The things I did made me ashamed. **I was truly repentant**, and was **willing to go in a complete opposite direction**. I didn't realize it yet, but this was the **first step of surrender to God**...yes, even in this twenty-first century. For the first time, my mind and heart opened to a new way of living.

I still did not understand yet (I would later), that we have a Lord who died for our sins, and that **anyone can ask for, and receive forgiveness** (this is necessary for restoration of rightness with our Creator-God). This forgiveness is provided by the sinless blood of Jesus.

As long as a person thinks they have it all together, whether it is with their money, profession, good looks, or good deeds, they will not able to see their need of being saved—this is called pride.

...all have sinned and fall short of the glory of God.

(Romans 3:23)

My numerous arrests between 1995 and 2008 were a giant clue to my brokenness. I was fortunate to have these alerts because many people go through life not having a shattering event to uproot their complacency. I am thoroughly convinced that these people, at their core, are not at a consistent level of peace and joy. This can only come from a relationship with their Maker.

CHAPTER 4

THE JOURNEY BEGINS–
COUNTY JAIL

*T*he revelation of my Lord was progressive. His reality (to me) began manifesting in the holding cell at Williamson County Jail. Sitting in that small cement room full of newly arrested women was not a pleasant experience in itself, but add the fact that I had just been sentenced to prison, and the whole scene was almost unbearable; I would not be leaving this time on a bail bond. I was in for a 5 year haul, or....so I thought.

As I sat in this holding cell, I was thankful for the fact I had entered that in-patient drug and alcohol treatment center on May 1, 2009. I was grateful to be sober as I sat there facing the reality of prison. My sister, Sylvia, had been encouraging me for years to enter a rehab center to get off the drugs. She even made the offer to pay for treatment while on the phone in a third-party conference call (which she arranged) with a rehab in another state. As I lay in bed with a mild concussion, and blood-colored eyes from one of many falls, I told them "No, thank you, I can't leave my dogs, and besides, doctors tell me I need those pills." I wasn't ready to surrender; making excuses, I rejected the idea.

The legal situation looked less and less promising for probation, and I did not want to go into prison addicted to those medications. As terrified as I was to go into a rehab and get off the pills, the thought of being inside a prison facility eliminating the deadly toxins of those medicines from my body was more terrifying.

The last legal situation "forced" me to take action (getting off the drugs). I would have avoided that decision otherwise. I truly believe I would still willingly be in that desperate addicted condition if the legal circumstances, brought on by choices I made, had not intervened to change my mind.

On that second day at that treatment center the drugs had started clearing from my mind and body. As the days went by, I began to realize how messed up (zombie-like) I had been on those medications. "Oh, my goodness...I am guilty!!"

I began to see that I played the lead role in the tragedies of my life. Yes, there had been other actors, but it was me who always had complete choice over the way the script was written.

I really thought I was innocent of the DWI charge because I had not been drinking. I thought that because I had been arrested for driving while taking my own prescription drugs, the law was wrong, and I was innocent. I had gone before the judge every month from

August to April proclaiming my innocence. I had changed lawyers 3 times, and spent thousands of dollars ($27,000 on attorney fees) in an effort to influence the courts to give me leniency.

After 30 days in rehab, I went back before the judge and pled guilty. The removal of this weight gave me a lightness that felt incredibly liberating. Friends with me that day in court said they saw a visible relaxation on my body as I stood before that judge and proclaimed the truth of my guilt. The judge set the date of sentencing 2 months later.

Spiritual laws began to work immediately. Even though I was completely unaware they existed, the spiritual laws of goodness (made by our Creator) began to come into effect. The district attorney of Williamson County took out the "deadly weapon" clause of my charge. The car was described by law to be a weapon because I was driving, again, under the influence of mood-altering substances. This clause would make it mandatory to serve half of any sentence time (if I got sentenced to prison) before I would be eligible for parole. The district attorney threw out this "deadly weapon" clause that even the $27,000 had failed to remove. The truth (my confession of guilt) had prevailed, and spiritual laws went to work in my behalf.

I went back to the in-patient rehab, and remained there until the appointed date (July 29, 2009).

I was driven from the treatment center directly to court the morning of my sentencing. I had 3 months of sobriety from the drugs, and my mind was very clear. It is a good thing I did not have the opportunity to go home beforehand because there were 2 large bottles of prescription drugs I had hidden under my mattress the day I entered rehab. My addictive mindset certainly did not hesitate to lie and tell my sister that I had flushed those xanax and vicodin pills down the toilet. In my sick thinking, I wanted to safeguard those drugs and keep them around.....just in case, maybe later?? (my sister later destroyed those pills).

The courtroom was filled with supportive friends (mainly from Alcoholics Anonymous and a few from church) the morning of the sentencing. My sister Sylvia had flown in from Oregon. It gave me encouragement that so many people had showed up in my behalf. Even though we were all there by 8:30 am, the sentencing did not take place until afternoon. I was terrified of going to prison, and was hoping for probation. I would have accepted 20 years probation (or more!) instead of prison.

As I stood in front of that judge and heard him pronounce a 5 year prison sentence, I was absolutely stunned; I don't think I even cried. I looked behind me, and most every one of those there for me was crying. My sister mouthed "I love you".

Being in bondage to any addiction is never a solo act; others are inadvertently affected in some way. **People we love always get hurt by our addictive lifestyles.**

Even though I had just been sentenced to 5 years prison, there was great relief on my part that at least now I knew what was going to happen. I had played out scenarios in my head many times during those 11 months leading up to this day. My thoughts had pretty much been consumed with fear and dread, resulting in a continual state of anxiety.

I was handcuffed, and carried away to county jail (which connected with the court building where I was sentenced). I was placed in a small, rectangular, cement holding cell until I could be assigned a more permanent cell on another floor. Everything in this holding cell was hard and cold—cement walls, floor, bench, and one exposed metal toilet; absolutely no privacy.

A holding cell is a temporary confinement room where every newly-arrested person is taken. You are placed here until release by bail bond, or until taken to another part of the jail.

After I had been sitting in this holding cell for a few hours, scared and miserable, a young woman came in. I do not remember how our conversation started as I did not feel very chatty, but it did, and in the course of it she revealed that she knew my next door neighbor Nancy. This young woman knew Nancy's grown kids, and had even been to her house. You might think this is not so unusual, but we live in another county (Travis) some 40 miles from this jail. Talking with this woman in the holding cell, who knew my next door neighbor and friend, gave me a comforting feeling. This might sound strange if you have never been in this situation; I was going to prison, and I want to tell you that this small thing was calming to me.

Later on, 2 women came in at separate times; both were there on a bench-warrant. This means they were taken out of another facility to satisfy some unsettled legal issue with Williamson County. They began talking to each other, and even though they were there from different TDCJ prison units, they were comparing prison life—the food, rules, guards, other inmates. After listening to them for awhile, I talked to each and asked questions about life in prison. This also made me more comfortable; here were 2 prison inmates, just regular women (moms, wives, daughters, sisters). They had been shattered early on by life circumstances, and eventually had broken a law trying to live out life in their own way.

A skeptic will say these incidents were coincidences. I have been in county holding cells more times than I can even remember, and nothing like this had ever happened before. I had never been in a holding cell and even talked to anyone to any great degree. This had my attention, but I had no idea that it was my Maker.

The revelation of our Creator God's nature was progressively revealed to me in a discernable way over the next few months of incarceration, but the month that I spent in Williamson County jail before being transported to prison, set a firm foundation on His reality.

After many grueling hours in that small, cramped holding cell, I was processed (which means I was given a county outfit to wear, fingerprinted, and many photos taken). I was then escorted to another floor. Upon entering the door of the cell where I would stay for the next few weeks, a young woman came up to me from the opposite side of the room. This woman told me she had been in the holding cell with me on the day of my arrest, 8/8/8. I did not remember her, but she recognized me from 11 months prior.

This particular cell held around 30 women, and amazingly, one of them had been in the holding cell with me on 8/8/8. As it turned out, she was to be my bunkmate. This very young woman was especially thoughtful and considerate in helping me adjust to this environment. My God was making me as comfortable as possible in this horrific situation.

I would later learn that one of the things our God does is give comfort to people in a very special way. It is not only what He does, it is a part of His very nature; He is comfort.

> *Blessed be the God and Father of our Lord Jesus Christ, the Father of mercies and God of all comfort, who comforts us in all our tribulation, that we may be able to comfort those who are in any trouble, with the comfort with which we ourselves are comforted by God. (2 Corinthians 1:3-4)*

There wasn't much to do in county jail. Most women slept, played cards, or read. It was in county jail that I first heard of Kenneth Copeland Ministries through their 'Believer's Voice of Victory' magazine. This magazine was mixed in with a stack of reading materials in that jail-dorm. I was drawn to read it; I could not have known then how much this ministry would help me.

It was also from this stack of reading materials that I looked through a devotional book. This book was arranged by dates, and so I looked at the birth date of my Granny Lou, August 3. I was quite surprised to read on that page the very same thing she had written in a Bible that she gave me upon my graduation from High School. It said something like "Sin will keep you from this Book, but this Book will keep you from sin". Amazing "coincidence"—huh?

I was in this cell for 2 weeks during which I put in for trustee status (just filling out a request form). This allowed me to leave the cell for 8 hours several days each week, to go to another part of the jail. Not that this is exciting in itself, but in a situation like this you learn to appreciate the very small things in life.

During one of the shifts as a trustee I was in another cell that housed women needing more supervision. It was my job to watch a woman accused of murder; to make sure she did not try to hurt herself. As I sat watching through the glass front of her cell, I glanced up at the window at the top of the ceiling, and there was this beautiful full moon right in my line of vision for about 5 minutes; I could not take my eyes off its brilliance.

The moon would later become a permanent source of comfort between the Lord and me as it signified that He, as the Creator of it, was somewhere out there beyond, and in control. The fact is, I was able to view a full moon every single month I was incarcerated. This is a miracle in itself when you are confined to a prison cell, and at the discretion of a guard whether you can go outside or not.

After a couple of weeks, I was moved to a trustee cell on another floor. This turned out to be a cell with only 2 other women inside; it opened to a common area which accommodated several inmate-packed cells.

For over 2 weeks I would be in this cell before I was transported to prison. It is hard to explain all of the events that took place during this time. There was a divine spiritual movement of such a pace that I did not know what was going on, but I knew it was personal. It is difficult to describe. I can only attempt to share a little of the divine spiritual whirlwind that took place during those last 2 weeks in county jail.

Many, many times when I was out in the common area, or on trustee duty, I met women who had a connection with my very own life.

I spent around 5 months in Williamson County Jail in 1997 for the intoxicated assault, and some of these women tied in to that period. I talked to one woman who had been incarcerated at that same time, and was in one of the cells I had been in. I would not have recognized her, but in conversation it became apparent that we had been cellmates. Another woman talked about her "colorful" relative being confined in Williamson County jail in 1997, and I clearly remembered her unusual name, and offensive sexual antics.

I met 2 women who currently knew people I know, in the Lake Travis area outside of Austin, Texas, where I live. One dated an old friend of mine, and one was best friends with someone I had worked for recently (for a brief time). One of the 2 trustees in my cell even knew an Alcoholic Anonymous sponsor, whose name and phone number were written in my AA book (that Sylvia had brought to me). It was her mother's best friend!

I wrote a friend, and tried to explain the bizarre happenings at that jail, but words can't adequately describe the reality of spiritual happenings. I even talked with the other 2 trustees about how this experience would make a good movie. I didn't understand it all, but my attention was captured. I definitely knew something was going on, and that it was coming from another realm, but I still did not have complete awareness that it was my Maker, communicating with me.

Would the Creator God talk to me?...YES! He was preparing my heart for the complete awareness that He is real, He is alive, and that He loves unconditionally in a very personal way.

...God is love. (1John 4:8)

Chapter 5

ON TO PRISON —TDCJ

The trip from Williamson Co. Jail to prison was unpleasant to say the least. I think there were nine of us handcuffed to each other and crammed into a van. I was handcuffed to a woman on each side of me, and we were in the back. We were tired as the van drove away from the jail around 2 am. All of us were scared of the unknown prison adventure, and eventually all small talk dwindled to silence.

At some point I turned my head to look out the back window, and there was a large, almost full, orangish-colored moon looming over the van. I smiled to myself as I remembered the full moon at the jail a few weeks back. I would glance back at the moon often on that trip, as if to get some sort of assurance that everything would be ok. God was behind the moon that He created. I wanted to believe He was watching over me, and....He was!

After about 5 hours, we arrived at Plane State Jail (prison) in Dayton, Texas. As we pulled up to the front of the prison, the moon was going down in the sky behind us, and an orange sun was coming up over the horizon in front of us. The end of one day is "A New Beginning" (the meaning of the number 8) of another. The date was September 2, 2009.

What a humbling experience the first day in prison turned out to be. I suppose the point is to show you are not in control of anything. This is what our Lord wants to get across to us as well, but there is a total, complete, difference in that He does not beat you down to make that point. Our Lord lets each person determine their own helplessness. He allows you to come to Him when you are weary, and when His assistance is sought. He is standing by, and ever ready to welcome you to Himself. Our Lord is more than happy to take your burden from you, to step in and direct your life for you. **It is up to you to let go of the self-deceiving pride that says you can do it by yourself.**

> *Therefore **humble yourselves** under the mighty hand of God, that He may exalt you in due time, casting all your care upon Him, for He cares for you. (1 Peter 5:6-7)*

59

*"**Follow My teachings** and learn from Me. **I am
gentle and do not have pride**. You will have rest for
your souls."* (*Matthew 11:29,* New Life Version)

Prison is not like our Lord. There are no welcoming arms to
make you know that you are loved. We were herded in like a bunch
of cattle going to market. It was freezing cold in the initial processing room. We had to strip off all our clothes, and perform some
humiliating physical positions to make sure nobody had brought
in contraband. The whole time there are several guards staring at
you, and screaming orders. Welcome to TDCJ (Texas Department
of Criminal Justice).

At the end of a very long day of an endless (seemingly) parade of
humiliating tasks to complete, you are assigned to one of many temporary cells. The inmates term these "The Dog Pound" because they
resemble wire cages stacked on top of one another. The cell I was
in had 8 bunk beds. It was dark in this area with minimal lighting,
and very few windows. The cell I was assigned did not have any
windows; I would not have known if it was day or night except by
the times that meals were served; breakfast around 3:30am, lunch
around 10:30am, and dinner around 3:30pm.

We were called out of our cell two at a time each day for a shower
of ice-cold water that was released by pressing a button over and
over. Also there was no air conditioning, and it was September—in

Texas. The accommodations would qualify for about a negative five-star rating. This was my "home" for 3 weeks.

During these 3 weeks, the only reading material allowed were TDCJ-issued manuals stating rules and regulations, and the Bible. TDCJ will allow inmates to enter with a Bible if brought from county jail (inmates can also get Bibles from the chaplain of the unit, or have someone send one by mail). I had a Bible that my sister, Sylvia, had taken to me at Williamson County at the same time she took my Alcoholics Anonymous 'Twelve-Step Big Book'.

I was not allowed to enter prison with the AA book, and have not really looked at one since county jail. I discovered the Bible, and the perfect Word of God (Jesus) removed the addiction of alcohol and drugs that over a decade of participation in the 12-step recovery program had not been able to do for me. The steps helped me to see that I had a thinking and heart problem, but they needed to be healed (not just acknowledged).

A "higher power" never relieved me of my addiction to alcohol and drugs…it took THE Highest Power of Jesus Christ to heal my inner pain. When He did this for me, all symptoms of addictive insanity were completely removed. **Lord Jesus Christ is a One-step program.**

> *For the **word of God is living and powerful**, and sharper that any two-edged sword, piercing even to the division of soul and spirit, and of joints and*

> marrow, **and is a discerner of the thoughts and intents of the heart**. *(Hebrews 4:12)*

I had never read the Bible, even though I had been given, and owned, more than one. They were just books to me. I kept them through the years because they had sentimental attachments. The Bible I took into prison was one that my sister had given me years before, and it was very easy to read and understand. It is called 'The Book'.

The processing that TDCJ does on new arrivals to prison provided me ample time in this darkish cell to lie on the bunk, and become acquainted with God's awesome Word. There was a young woman in the bunk next to mine that gave me a list of her 20 favorite books of the Bible (I still have the list). Her list included both Old and New Testament books. I began reading from her list, and then I read more.

I could not understand the Bible yet, but even my superficial reading of it began planting God's Word as seed in my heart. It would, in time, be ready to produce in my life...one day soon.

> ...**born again**, *not of corruptible seed but incorruptible, through the word of God which lives and abides forever. (1 Peter 1:23)*

Of course I still did not know any of this. I did not realize yet how the Word of God could (and would) eventually determine the direction my life went. In total honesty, I was just passing time, and seeking distraction in the present lousy situation. One day while reading, a verse really stood out to me. It just sort of opened up in meaning.

Later, I would find out that God often uses verses in scripture to speak individually to your heart. The first verse He ever talked to me through was Proverbs 20:24. I did not know at that time He was talking to me, but I definitely knew the verse stood out; it took on a special, personal significance.

A man's steps are of the Lord; How then can a man
understand his own way? (Proverbs 20:24)

It was in reading the Bible, and spending time with God, that I began understanding the truth; Jesus Christ is the Son of God. My choices had forced me into this situation where I had nothing else to do but read the Bible. Ironically, I actually was blessed by this time; I don't think I would have ever taken the initiative to read the Bible on my own. It takes alone time with God and His Word to learn about Him, about His Son, and about yourself.

CHAPTER 6

DORM C

*T*he day came that I was called to be moved to another building. I had been taken out of that "cage environment" a few times during those first 3 weeks for various testing. The prison system is quite thorough with their evaluation of an inmate's physical and mental health, education level, and emotional stability. Although the testing (written, oral, and medical) was done in different areas of the prison unit, I was still not familiar with the entire prison.

On the day of transfer to my permanent dorm, I carried my mattress and personal belongings down the center of Plane State (which inmates call Main Street). The realization that this was to be my residence for 5 years flooded my being with dread. As I viewed all of the prison buildings lining both sides of Main Street, I was not a happy camper.

The large square metal building I was assigned had 4 dorms in it (one in each corner), with a guard station in the middle. The 4 dorms each had a glass in the front, which allowed the guards on duty to have partial view into them.

As I stood at the door to Dorm C, I could see inside through the glass. I was assigned a dorm with 56 women (28 bunk beds). I was not even through the door when one of them rushed over to help me with my mattress. This seemed like a nice gesture, but in reality it is rare for an inmate to do something nice for another inmate in prison without wanting something in return. I did not know that yet. Lessons came quickly, and I learned fast that the best place to stay was on my bunk bed.

The bunk bed I was assigned would have been the one chosen, if I would have had a choice. All bunk beds were arranged around a center area, with absolutely no privacy, except for 2 bunks which were in a sort of alcove-like corner, and I was assigned one of these. Out of these two, the one assigned to me had a view of a window. Even though this window was high up on the wall, and painted white, it did afford knowledge of day or night. I value both privacy and windows. I was also assigned the lower bunk—a huge blessing. It is not so much fun to climb in and out of your bed by a ladder when you are 55 years old.

I know that our personal God is very thoughtful about taking into consideration our individual preferences, and He accommodates us by allowing them to manifest in our lives—even in prison.

Delight yourself in the Lord and He will give you the desires of your heart. (Psalm 37:4)

It is an amazing fact that after I met my Lord, His desires started becoming my desires.

My bunk was across from the bunk of a woman who had come in the van with me from Williamson County. She said something quite horrific before leaving that jail, and I thought to myself that I would stay away from her. As it turned out, she was in the first cell with me in the "dog pound", and now here she was again within 3 feet of my bunk. This is highly unusual since Plane State is a very large women's unit. The probability this would happen is very unlikely, unless... it was by Divine appointment.

I did not know it then, but this woman would become my best friend in prison. Her name was Melissa. As it turned out, I left prison before her, but wrote to her almost weekly, and put some money in her prison account on a regular basis.

Our God knows things that we can't know, and He uses this knowledge to do great things for His kingdom purposes.

'I was naked and you clothed Me; I was sick and you visited Me; I was in prison and you came to Me.' (Matthew 25:36)

This was Jesus talking to His disciples, and telling them by doing these things it would be pleasing to Him. It would be as if they were doing it for Him. This is the Lord's heart, and in helping Melissa out of the love I developed for her, I was in the will of my Lord.

As I settled into the resigned fact that I was in prison for awhile, I decided to take a course or two to pass time outside of the dorm. This unit offered several Christian classes, and the first one I tried to get into was recommended by someone in Dorm C. I thought I would try, but did not really think I would get into it.

In prison everything is done by paperwork. Requests are submitted by inmates through "I-60s" (these are turned in at guard stations). Directions to inmates are through "lay-ins". A lay-in is required for movement in prison, as it specifies where the inmate is going, and at what time (these are passed out by the guards). Everything has to be assigned, and approved by prison hierarchy, and the usual response time is lengthy.

The class recommended to me was not easy to get in because it was popular with inmates, and always filled to capacity by demand. Amazingly, I was able to get in right away, and my first Monday night class began the week after my I-60 submittal. Called Davis' Disciples, it met each Monday night.

I didn't know what to expect from this class. Pastor Davis turned out to be a charming man. He did not allow his college degree, or seminary training, to interfere with the way he interacted with the inmates. He instructed in a way in which they could relate. He did not teach from a level of superiority, he taught so they would understand what he was saying.

That first night, I witnessed a demonstration of genuine concern for those inmates. I observed this in the way he answered an inmate's question. I do not remember what she asked, or what he answered, but I do remember knowing his response came from realness in his heart.

Pastor Henry Lee Davis opened up the Bible in a way that stimulated my desire to study more. This was the first time to hear these wonderful things he taught, and I was delighted to learn that the Bible is an amazing and fascinating book (more than just a way to pass time).

Since that time, I have been an avid student of the Bible, seeking out delicious treasures held between its pages. It was through my reading of God's Word that I began to know the reality of Jesus Christ as the Son of God.

I was learning of the character and nature of our living Lord. I was beginning to be familiar with Him, and to rely on His presence to get me through each day. Prison life is very dark, and although the Holy Spirit of God is all over the place, so are demonic spirits. Pretty much on a daily basis I would hear, or see, something that I could only attribute to sheer forces of evil. The saving grace of Lord Jesus Christ waltzed me through that horrific experience.

There were church services every Sunday in the prison chapel. Each week a different ministry would come to preach the good news of our Lord. Chapel services were filled with inmates each week, and though many went seeking the Answer to their broken lives, some inmates went for their own distorted amusement.

I went each Sunday to find out exactly who my God was, seeking His permanent remedy for my own brokenness. Bible studies, personal encounters, and Sunday messages all confirmed an awesome God. I wanted to know what His will was for me, and what He wanted from me.

During those weeks of Sunday services, salvation prayers were offered to afford the inmates opportunity to get right with our God, through surrender to Lord Jesus Christ. I knew that God was very real, and that He was working in my life in a very personal way. Even though I did not have a clear idea of Him yet, I knew enough to want to be reborn as His child. I wanted to be with God eternally.

In rehab, I came to that point in life a lot of people want to skip... **repentance**. I accepted responsibility for my part in the scheme of sin. I did not know at the time (in rehab), I was taking the necessary first step (repentance), to experience God's **eternal grace**. Now, here I was in prison, ready to take the next step...**surrender** to Jesus.

I was truly repentant for my errors, and I sincerely humbled myself (from my heart) before the living God. I asked for His help. I wanted Jesus to take over my broken life.

"See, O Lord, how distressed I am! I am in torment within, and in my heart I am disturbed, for I have been most rebellious... (Lamentations 1:20, NIV)

There is no "formula" salvation prayer that will save on its own. It is only in saying sincere, heartfelt words of surrender to Jesus (with genuine inner belief that He is the Son of God), that will provide salvation. Our God knows the difference between a person's genuine bowing of their heart, or if someone is just going through the motion of saying words.

.. if you confess with your mouth the Lord Jesus and believe in your heart that God raised Him from the dead, you will be saved. For with the heart one believes unto righteousness, and with the mouth confession is made unto salvation. (Romans 10:9-10)

CHAPTER 7

A CHANGE IS COMING

*I*n November, TDCJ had one of its yearly lockdowns. I never really knew what this was all about, but it involved 5 days of dorm confinement. You are ordered to stay on your bunk, and meals are brought to you in paper sacks. The first morning of lockdown, I woke up very early, sat up on my bunk, and **I knew that I was different**.

As I looked around the room, a love for these women was alive in my heart. I was stunned at my own sentiments because these women were not all visibly lovable. For a brief moment I was confused as to why I was having these feelings, but very shortly I would realize that this was unmistakable confirmation of the Holy Spirit's tangible manifestation in my heart. I had been spiritually reborn a child of God, in His nature, and this change was astonishingly recognizable in my life. Wow!

...the love of God has been poured out in our hearts by the Holy Spirit who was given to us. (Romans 5:5)

On one of the beginning days of lockdown, each inmate had to put their belongings in mesh bags, and carry them to the dining hall to be inspected. When you have books and commissary items to tote, as well as the prison mattress and sheets, things get heavy. It is a dreaded yearly event that had the attention of every inmate.

The real amazing thing is that while packing up my stuff, I sat down and shared commissary food with a woman who had been in and out of prison most of her adult life. I had intentionally avoided this woman, and now I was offering my food to her. This in itself gave testimony to the new me. I have to say this was strange because I was the one it was happening to, and it was very real!

> *... if anyone is in Christ, he is a new creation; old things have passed away; behold, all things have become new. (2 Corinthians 5:17)*

A very wonderful thing happened the afternoon of the day I awoke transformed by the Holy Spirit. When mail was brought in that afternoon, someone had sent me a journal. This journal allowed me to write down and record all of the awesome things that were happening. I later found out that my friend Patsy sent the journal. I wrote in it almost daily, and to this day I enjoy reading what I wrote during my journey in prison with the Lord I met there. I continue to journal daily about my walk in the Lord's kingdom. It is important to record things as they occur, so that time will not fade, or erase the memory.

That night I woke to find a lay-in on my bed, telling me that I was to report to G building to see a parole interviewer. During the initial first 3 week's evaluations, I was told I would see parole in March 2010. This was November 18, 2009 (4 months early). I took my lay-in and went at 8am to the parole interview which might enable me to leave prison before 5 years.

TDCJ is hard on DWIs, and because this was my fourth, I was informed by other inmates I would not go home on the first interview. I was told I would have to stay in prison at least until the second interview (which would occur 1 year later).

The interview was not a pleasant experience because many questions were asked about my years of addictions. It is not easy to relive a broken life of mistakes. I had been arrested not only for the DWIs, but numerous P.I.s (public intoxications, in restaurants where the police were called because of my drunken behavior), and a shop-lifting charge that occurred during one of my drunken shopping trips (a purse full of money and credit cards…I stole for the "thrill" of it). Not a pretty picture; in fact, a very ugly one! I made it through the interview, and would hope for a miracle.

A very interesting vision occurred to me one day as I was walking down the middle of Plane State to the dining hall. On this unit there were not many live plants to look at, but a row of bushes was planted in front of the education building. The leaves had fallen off; the bushes were bare, as it was late in the season. As I walked passed them on the way to the dining hall, the vision was very clear that when these bushes were green with new leaves of life, I would be going home. This was a very pleasant vision to think about, and I did meditate often on this over the following months. Frequently, as I passed by the dead bushes in front of that building, I would see it with green leaves.

> *...the vision is yet for an appointed time; but at the end it will speak, and it will not lie. Though it tarries, wait for it; because it will surely come...(Habakkuk 2:2-3)*

Soon after my spiritual awakening, I said a prayer asking complete immersion (baptism) of the Holy Spirit. This gives power to the rebirth of God's nature. It is a release of "self" into the authority of our Lord's ways (Jesus as Lord). I found out about this belief through reading a book by Kenneth and Gloria Copeland. I had never heard this through religious teachings, but I sure wanted the fullness of what my God had for me. I absolutely believe that the intentional relinquishing of "self" to the Holy Spirit is the reason I began experiencing Lord Jesus in such a powerful way.

Around this time I became intensely aware of the presence of God. His living presence inside me was so very perceptible that I was extremely self-conscious when in the bathroom performing personal duties. This was bizarre, but very real—I was not alone. This went on for several days. How very extraordinary this was to me, but how very wonderful. I marvel to this day that I was able to experience the blissful reality of His presence in such a tangible way. Wow!

The fact is, His presence is that strong with each true believer, and is only hampered by their awareness of Him. Focus to any problem on this earth will restrict, even prevent this awareness of our living God. All true believers (having surrendered to Jesus) have God's Holy Spirit dwelling inside; they are His temple.

> ...*your body is the temple of the Holy Spirit who is in*
> *you, whom you have from God...(1 Corinthians 6:19)*

I have not recaptured that tangible depth of awareness since those days in prison. Obviously, I have allowed my center of attention to vacillate between His Truth inside me, and issues of the outside world. I hold the memory close in my heart, with hope of recapturing that tangible consciousness of His presence.

It wasn't long before God started to work on me about my pride. I knew He was talking to me about it, but I didn't think I was particularly prideful. I asked Him to show me what He meant. It got to where I could not open my mouth without Holy Spirit pointing out that my words were prideful...Ouch! Their focus frequently centered on me, instead of pointing toward Him—"What I thought", "What I did", "What I wanted", instead of "What He thinks", "What He does", and "What He wants".

Also Holy Spirit pointed out to me that I seemed obsessed with looking in the mirror. I had no idea I did that. TDCJ mirrors are scratched up pieces of metal (not glass), and it was quite an awakening to me that I would glance at one every time I passed by even though I could not see myself clearly. The thing is, I looked at myself at every opportunity as I walked by any glass that would give me a reflection.

This had to stop, and I started making conscious efforts not to look. My obsession with my looks did not begin in prison. The world, erroneously, makes physical looks so important that I began to try and "smooth out" a couple of perceived physical flaws. During my late twenties and thirties, I **foolishly** put myself through a few plastic surgery procedures. These weren't necessary; infact, most people who knew me would not have noticed that I even had these **vain** surgeries.

I still make mindful choices to this day about looking in every mirror I pass by. Do I look any different that I looked 5 minutes before?....I don't think so!

The holiday season came, and Christmas was very special to me for the first time. I was full of joy in having a new relationship with the One (Lord Jesus Christ) who should be the only focus. Considering that it was prison, TDCJ did a good job of making the main meal special. Some inmates were in a festive mood, but many more of them were depressed because they had families that would be celebrating without them. The majority of women in prison have kids, and many of these are very young children. Prison is an extremely tragic and indisputable reality of broken families, broken homes, broken dreams—-broken lives.

On Christmas day, some inmates in the dorm put on a sort of variety show. The fact is that prisons are filled with very talented people. With so much to offer the world, it is unfortunate that these people have bought into the deceptive lies of unworthiness. These lies (from the devil) ushered them into prison….they don't know how valuable they are (creations of the living God). Most of the talent show Christmas day involved singers, and I was asked by one of the "headliners" to sit on the front bench in a place of honor.

Now this was an unexpected surprise, as the invitation was extended by an inmate I had never talked to. Her bunk was across the dorm, and there were undesirable sexual activities taking place there on a regular basis. Apparently, for some reason, I had been observed to her approval.

The thing is, people naturally watch other people. Christians are being observed, and evaluated, even when they are unaware of this fact. A person who walks with the Lord is on stage subject to critique, and the performance is everyday. Everywhere a Christian goes they are performing, and hopefully demonstrating the Lord's love nature.

> *...we are to God the fragrance of Christ among those who are being saved and among those who are per-ishing. To the one we are the aroma of death leading to death, and to the other the aroma of life leading to life...(2 Corinthians 2:15-16)*

On New Year's Day I began reading the Bible using a year-long plan from a 'Daily Bread' devotional that had been passed out in one of the Sunday services. I wanted to read from Genesis to Revelation so I could understand the true meaning of His Word. I would read for myself what God said. Comprehension of the entire Book is only obtained by a thorough reading, and studying, of the complete Bible. The Old and New Testaments are intertwined to form a complete picture. A person can make God's Word say pretty much anything they want it to by taking scripture out of context. Unfortunately, this is done all of the time.

I was using a Bible sent to me by a woman from Rusk, Texas. I got her name from an inmate, and wrote to her requesting a new Bible. I wanted one that would help me study scripture more in-depth than the one I had brought into prison. This wonderful woman (in ministry to help inmates) complied by sending a (NKJV) New Spirit Filled Life Bible. It was a Bible that gave a lot of information about scripture, including elaborations on Hebrew and Greek words. This Bible really helped me to understand scripture (today it is still my core Bible).

I was reading a morning devotional one day and when I read Acts 27:25, the Lord spoke to me, and I knew I was going home on the first parole.

...take heart, men, for I believe God, that it will be just as it was told me. (Acts 27:25)

No, this verse does not say I would go home on my first parole, but God said this to my heart through this verse. This was the second time He spoke to me through scripture. I was a novice at hearing the living God talk to me, but I knew that He just did. Through this verse His voice was audible in my heart...unmistakably, I heard it!

I could not figure out how the parole board would vote to let me go home on my first parole interview because my arrest record was long and ugly. That arrest for the third DWI in 1996 was an intoxication assault; kids had been injured in that accident. This incident alone would impress upon the parole board that I had not learned from my past mistakes.

Yes, I had changed, and yes, I had repented of my sins and surrendered to Lord Jesus Christ, but the parole board only knew me by what the black and white print said about me on my arrest reports (nevertheless God knew). There might be some positive comments made by the parole interviewer back in November, but that woman had told me that she was not a voter on my case. Without meeting and talking to me firsthand, how could the board know that I was worth the risk of being released to go home on parole?

That is where my living God comes to the rescue. He can make things happen that, to the world who does not know Him, seem quite impossible.

> *...Jesus looked at them and said to them, "With men this is impossible, but with God all things are possible." (Matthew 19:26)*

As the weeks of January passed, I reflected on these things quite often. Inmates certainly liked to have their input about how the parole board would not grant me parole until maybe the next year, when I would be eligible for another interview. A good portion of inmates have been in prison several times over a period of years, and they are "experts" on the legal system (having both experienced and witnessed it). The fact was,there were many women in prison for 3 or 4 DWIs, and everyone I talked with (having received their answer back from parole), was waiting another year to be reviewed, again.

I had been told, back in November, I would have my answer in about 4 months. This was January, thus giving me another couple of months to come up with scenarios on how God would make what He had told me (through Acts 27:25) come to pass. I never doubted what He had told me. My walk with Him had not been contaminated by religious unbelief, and my faith in His Word was pure and strong.

I held tight to my inner belief that He told me I would go home on the first parole.

At the end of January, I awoke to find another lay-in on my bed telling me I was to report to building G to see parole. I assumed this was my official TDCJ answer 2 months early. I was calm because I knew what God had told me.

Before I left the dorm, I was in the bathroom and a Michael Jackson song kept playing in my head. The tune and the words, "just call out my name and I'll be there" played over and over in my head. Even though I was familiar with the song, it was not one that I ever thought of. It was such an odd thing to be hearing this tune in my head. All of the sudden, I realized my Lord Jesus Christ was saying that faith in His powerful name would assure me strength and victory amidst any, and all, circumstances.

> *"...His name, through faith in His name, has made this man strong, whom you see and know. Yes, the faith which comes through Him has given him this perfect soundness in the presence of you all."* *(Acts 3:16)*

When I arrived at G building, other inmates in line told me that we would be seeing the parole commissioner. I certainly did not understand why I would be seeing a commissioner, but would definitely ask when I got inside.

It was over an hour before I was called inside for my appointment. This gave me ample time to ponder why a parole commissioner would be seeing me. Apparently, they do not come onto units very often. The commissioner turned out to be a woman. I asked why I was seeing her, and she told me she had picked my file up off her desk that morning **"at random".** As it turned out, she would be the lead voter on my case. This presented the opportunity for the lead voter to get acquainted with the person in the file.

So this is how my lovely Lord God worked that out. He has a million ways to do things, and quite frequently, it is not like anything we could dream up.

> ...the Lord said to Moses, "Has the Lord's arm been shortened? Now you shall see whether what I say will happen to you or not." (Numbers 11:23)

She told me I would have the parole's answer in 2 weeks. I already had God's answer. I woke up to another lay-in a couple days later. This one told me I would be going to a prison class called Changes, starting the next day. This class is indicative that an inmate is going home.

It is difficult to convey the excitement of knowing the Creator God has stepped into the earthly realm (on my behalf) with His divine providence. The realization that the God of the universe was at work to influence my personal fate is beyond human words. "I'm going home, I'm going home, and...God Almighty had made it happen!" Hallelujah!

I began that class in the first couple of days in February. The class is about 4 months long. I got my "official TDCJ" answer within a week of beginning that class, and the paperwork gave a release date of June 2010.

The official TDCJ answer, that I would go home, was given to me 2 months earlier than I was supposed to have had my first parole interview. Thank you Lord Jesus. Wow!

CHAPTER 8

REAL CHANGE COMES FROM A PERSON

The Changes class was at 8am Monday through Friday. There were about 30 women in this particular class. The class is designed to help inmates make necessary alterations before leaving the prison unit. Adjustments to life, outside of prison, can be traumatic if the issues bringing the inmate into prison are not addressed.

Everyone was glad to be in this class, in the sense that it meant going home; unfortunately, this alone did not eliminate bad attitudes. Disrespect from the inmates toward the instructor, and each other, made for a tense atmosphere. The noise level of talking was disturbing to the point of intolerance. Dorm C, where I was housed, was like this all day and half the night, but I expected that a classroom setting would be more sedate.

The sad fact was, many of the women had a blatant contempt for life in general. There were no happy-at-home life stories in prison.

The majority of these women had lives that fostered self-preservation in any way they could manage. The various ways devised for survival on this earth were the very things escorting them into prison. A wide variety of survival methods included prostitution, drug usage and/or sales, theft, and many, many others.

The root of brokenness, branching off into desperation, was common in these various attempts to attain a better life. These women suffered from a feeling that they were unloved, and unlovable. Something bad began to happen to each one of them at a very young age.

The sad thing is that most of these women had children who would probably be influenced to devise their own survival methods. It was common for inmates to be the second, or third, generation in a line of family members sent to prison. Broken people break other people. It is a cycle of captivity that needs to be destroyed. There is only One who can free the captive permanently, and completely — our Lord Jesus Christ. I know this first-hand because He did it for me...real change does not come from a class, but from a Person.

The negative performances displayed by my parents definitely had a strong impact on my own choices (I did have choices). Dysfunctional behaviors took me captive as I brought them to fruition in my own life. I uncannily kept the destructive cycle in motion. I could never have been persuaded that re-creation of some of their bizarre conduct would put me in prison.

Even my suicide attempts likely stemmed from a subliminal message (implanted in me when my mom tried to end her life)..."My life is worthless. I'm tired of trying, I'll end this misery!" I was around seven when she slit her wrists.

I retain dramatic recollections of blood pouring on the floor as my dad and granny tore a white sheet in strips. These strips were wound tightly around the gashes so my mother could be taken to the hospital emergency. "Why did my mommy do that—doesn't she love me?" "Will mommy die?" "Where is Daddy taking her?" "Will my mommy come back?"

I suppose my mother's pain was so intense she tried to eliminate it by taking her life. You would think I would have learned from this horrific experience, so as not to replicate it. There are exceptions of course, but quite frequently, deep-rooted behavior is acted out without contemplation.

I insanely tried to manage life using the same patterns I had seen growing up. I convinced myself I was handling life in a completely different way than my parents. For decades, I could not see the parallel. It took Jesus to break through these old mind-sets, and completely liberate me.

> *...He has sent Me to heal the brokenhearted, **to proclaim liberty to the captives**, and the **opening of the prison to those who are bound**; (Isaiah 61:1)*

Masks of pride are handed down like family heirlooms. They feel comfortable (at first) because they have been around so long. Family members just slip right into them like old worn slippers. These barriers of protection have been carefully devised by pieces of world philosophy (me, me, me), and positioned to shield against invasion of potential hurt by someone else.

Every mask of pride is held in place by bands of unforgiveness, resentment, entitlement, and fear. This uncomfortable garment will be discarded when a person gets revelation of who they really are, and how very much they are loved by their Maker. Minds can be renewed to the Truth, and lives changed, through reading the Bible. The awareness learned from God's Word will furnish a totally new wardrobe of comfortable clothing;...*as **God's chosen people, holy and dearly loved** clothe yourselves with compassion, kindness, humility, gentleness and patience and **over all these virtues put on love** which binds them all together in perfect unity. (Colossians 3: 12, 14*, NIV)

What happens if you don't change outfits? I personally witnessed a woman leaving prison, only to return pregnant a few months later. This is a perfect example of how wearing the same outfit, and attending the same "parties" can escalate problems. Lord Jesus desires to assist as a personal valet who dresses you in the perfect attire for each occasion that arises, but....you have to invite Him.

I wore that uncomfortable pride costume (me, me, me) for so long that it didn't fit anymore. I had woken up in prison wearing a new outfit of love. Did it ever feel good! Holy Spirit of Jesus would begin teaching me what accessories went well with it.

Every week, the Changes class offered opportunities to work on some aspect of life that could be a problem area needing to be addressed. I give credit to this class for these openings inviting Jesus to heal. No, this class is not spiritual, but by exposing areas needing repair, inmates become vulnerable and just might ask for Divine help.

The week dealing with uncovering family secrets revealed to me something that had been buried inside, and poisoning me, since I was a small child. Some incidents are so painful that they have been buried and seemingly non-existent, but....in reality they are alive, and hiding out in the dark places of one's mind.

These hidden incidents will ultimately manifest themselves to the world in a clever disguise of bad habits and behavior. The manifestations of hurt and pain do not have to lead to a governmental prison system, but will definitely imprison the person in their own head. A few of these could be overeating, overworking, gambling, pornography/sexual obsession, adultery, compulsive shopping, control issues, anger issues, etc...(accessories to the pride outfit).

I dealt with this remembered incident (indirect sexual molestation) by writing a letter to the offending person (a family member, but not a parent). This person had passed off the earth years before, and I told them in the letter how despicable their act was, but that I had forgiven them. By forgiving them, I freed myself from this poison to my soul. It is strange how this works, but it does. The forgiveness was not for them, but for me.

> "... *if you forgive men their trespasses, your heavenly Father will also forgive you." (Matthew 6:14)*

Father God forgave me for everything, once I prayed and asked Jesus to be my Lord and Savior. If I can be forgiven for all the mess I made, I can forgive others....*as Christ forgave you, so you must also do. (Colossians 3:13).*

I was free of the poison bitterness, held inside by the unresolved anger, of what this person had done. Unforgiveness is like taking poison to kill the other person. By forgiving, I put myself in a position to receive the blessings meant by God that would otherwise be restricted by pent-up unforgiveness.

As the weeks passed in this Changes class, I heard many very sad and tragic stories from these women. They had an early, and consistent, lifestyle of dysfunction that brought them to the point of sabotaging their own life.

Deep pain quite often manifests itself in very undesirable masks. Keeping a guard over my own attitudes and reactions to things on this earth should keep me busy, not allowing me time to evaluate others....*why do you judge your brother? Or why do you show contempt for your brother? For we must all stand before the judgment seat of Christ. (Romans 14:10).*

Holy Spirit, through this class, was teaching me to have more tolerance and compassion with those around me. I would try to get to know the person behind the mask — sometimes a daunting task.

Actually, I would find myself putting on the pride mask many times over the next years. "Parties" on earth often appeared the perfect occasion to wear one of these uncomfortable masks of pride. This type of disguise not only suffocates the wearer, but everyone around breathes its noxious fumes. When I find myself trying on the pride mask again, I try to remove it quickly, so that I can draw in a thankful breath of life.

CHAPTER 9

THE END IS NEAR

As spring approached, I kept watch on those bushes in front of the education building. I clearly had the vision of leaving when they had green leaves. The days were warm and sunny, but no new leaves were appearing on the bushes; then, one day,...the leafless bushes were gone. The bushes had been dug up, and the beds had new mulch spread on them. It appeared that new bushes would be put in. My vision had been that when they were green with life, I would be leaving Plane State. This was the middle part of March, and my release date was June.

Everyday I expected the new bushes to be in place when I passed the education building, but day after day the beds remained empty.

Time was not passing fast enough to suit me. It was becoming hot, and this unit of TDCJ did not have air conditioning. As the weeks passed, and temperatures rose, so did the tempers of inmates. I saw more than one fight where women were escorted from dorm

C in handcuffs. I stayed on my bunk all of the time that I was in the cell.

To relieve the heat, I frequently poured cups of water over my head to drench myself; this was TDCJ air conditioning. Some inmates began to walk around in their underwear, and even though this was strictly against TDCJ rules, most guards ignored this out of some sort of compassion. This cell was in a metal building that had closed, painted windows, a reverse fan in the ceiling, and two small rotational fans placed high up on opposite walls. Like I said earlier, the rating would be a minus five-star.

Not everyone in the dorm was excited that I was being released. My bunkmate, Solma, was not pleased that she wasn't the one going home. She had been in prison several times, and had already been on Plane State unit for a long time with a burglary conviction. She was unpleasant to me, and quite often said very dark and ugly things about life in general.

One day a tall, large-framed woman came to me and said she had spoken to Solma about me. I was very surprised because I had never said much to this woman, except maybe an occasional "hello". I had avoided her because of the somewhat imposing attitude she presented. This woman, who called herself Deano, told Solma "If you lay a hand on Susan, you will have to answer to me!"

This created a fearful impact on Solma, and she restrained from talking to me at all, but... Solma's attitude toward me did not change; her lack of remarks was replaced with gestures. Some of the inmates saw Solma make signs behind my back indicating she would like to do me harm. These inmates finally wrote a letter to one of the sergeants, saying they feared Solma would hurt me. I began praying to God to please move her into another dorm.

I was called out of the dorm one night, about midnight, to talk to this sergeant. I was asked if I feared for my life, if I was scared of Solma. I had to say "No, I can't say I fear for my life, but I do believe she has an anger issue that could escalate into violence". The sergeant said TDCJ could do nothing if I didn't file an official complaint.

It was 2:30am, and I was walking down a deserted "main street", back to the dorm from the sergeant's office. I was crying (literally), and telling God "I don't understand why she wasn't moved out of the dorm". Later that afternoon, around 4pm, my bunkmate's name was called, "Solma, bunk number 34, pack up your stuff". She was to be moved off the Plane State Unit the very next day!

I jumped off my bunk, shouted with amazement, and danced around that dorm with my arms held high. "Our God is awesome!"He gives His children a shield of protection. He is ever mindful of our requirements, and has His loving guard over our lives twenty-four hours a day.

Our Creator knows what is in the heart, and mind, of each of His creations (what was in Solma's?), and desires to lead them in His path of righteousness. God was not only watching out for my interests; He knew what was best for Solma, and was working with

93

His loving touch, to protect her from possible reactions (toward me/ others), provoked by past hurts in her life.

It was amazing to watch the Creator of the universe working in my life, demonstrating Himself in a personal way through everyday things. It is as if He were "winking" at me, continually giving personal affirmation of His realness.

There was a table in the dorm where inmates put books they had finished reading. On a trip to the bathroom one night, I glanced toward this table. I had rarely, if ever, looked at the book selection on this table, because my focus was on reading the Bible. Why now, especially in the middle of the night, when things are going on in the dorm I did not want to see, did I glance at the table? I saw a single book on the table, and proceeded to walk over to see what it was. The book was 'Discover Your Destiny' by Charles Stanley. I picked it up and carried it to the bunk; this man was my Granny Lou's favorite pastor. My granny had passed in 1998, and I missed her very much. She had sent me a couple of Charles Stanley's books before she departed for heaven—those remained at home unread.

Even though I had never bothered to read the books my granny sent me, I began reading this one later that day. When I got to page 104, there was a sentence that told about a little girl telling her grandmother, Granny Lou, that she loved her, and that Jesus loved her too. Wow!

Even though I knew my Granny Lou loved God, she never shared that personal relationship with me. I saw her go to church, teach Sunday School, and write checks to the church. She had given me spiritual reading material, including a Bible. I don't doubt that she prayed **for** me often, although she never prayed **with** me. These are good things, but cannot replace demonstration of personal relationship with Jesus.

I'll never know why she didn't share about Him with me—maybe she was uncomfortable doing so. Her witness could have been the very thing influencing me to make right choices. A personal witness (can be as simple as praying with someone), can be the powerful stimuli prompting another to seek Jesus.

One of the highlights for me during those last months was the Davis' Disciple class on Monday nights. This class had been very encouraging and inspirational to me during all the months at Plane State. I looked forward to it each week in anticipation of learning something from Pastor Henry Lee Davis, a man I perceived as having a close personal relationship with the Lord. He not only taught from the Word, he demonstrated that he was a doer of God's Word—walking in love, compassion, wisdom, and knowledge. The Lord Jesus Christ shined through him in the midst of this dark prison environment.

> *...children of God without blemish (faultless, unre-bukable) in the midst of a crooked and wicked generation [spiritually perverted and perverse], among whom you are seen as bright lights (stars or beacons*

95

shining out clearly) in the [dark] world. (Philippians 2:15, AMP)

By the end of May I had finished the Changes class, and was just waiting around to be informed of a specific release date (all I knew so far was that I was leaving in June). Inmates call this "short-timing" because there is a lot of emotion going on inside a person who is leaving prison. Yes, the excitement is very high, but for most inmates there is a fear of the unknown outside those prison walls. For me, there was no fear because I had a good support group of friends and family, I owned a house, I had money in the bank to get me comfortably through a couple of years, and best of all, I had the Spirit of God living on the inside of me. The fact that I was walking out of prison with the living Holy Spirit, as resident in my heart, was going to make my transition to the outside a fairly easy one.

I knew that God had, supernaturally, removed any future desire for alcohol or drugs. I had the blissful freedom found only in Christ. It was my decision to give my life to Him, and when I did He removed that addiction of drugs and alcohol from me. He set me free from this bondage of death. I had tried to quit many times, but the day always came when all resolutions to stop would be thrown out.

One would think the eight months spent in court-appointed county confinement (1997) would cure me of the desire of alcohol and drugs. During those eight months, my body was certainly purged of those substances, but....the desire to continue using those toxic, mind-altering substances never left me (the problem was inside). In fact, I used pills and alcohol the very day I got out. It was my birthday, and "I needed to have a good time on my forty-third year", and "I needed to celebrate the fact that I was free after 8 months of county confinement".

So many things seem to trigger the urge to drink, or do drugs—a good day, a bad day. The world tries to make the use of these look glamorous as a way to celebrate, or soothing as a way to relax, but.... there is nothing attractive about being drunk and handcuffed.

There is no star quality in hurting your family and friends, over and over, until they have a hard time trusting you. The story of drugs and alcohol plays out as a very sad and tragic drama that guarantees no academy award winning salaries. In fact, a person headlining in this drama has to pay big to star in it...*the wages of sin is death, but the Gift of God is Eternal Life in Christ Jesus our Lord. (Romans 6:23).*

I knew that I was free of this hideous life-style of trying to fill the void in my soul. Like I said, the Spirit of Lord Jesus was in residence now, and had replaced the emptiness with Love that I never knew was possible.

Those last few weeks of prison, I went outside into the recreation yard as many times as the guards allowed. It was good to be getting fresh air while giving praise, out loud, to my Lord Jesus Christ that I was leaving the prison system behind (only 10 ½ months of a 5 year sentence—Wow! Wow! Wow!). The recreation yard is where I was able to see a full (according to my eyes) moon each month that I was in prison.

There were no set times for the recreation yard. It could be at eight in the morning, four in the afternoon, nine at night, or any hour in between. This privilege was given a few times each week, not everyday; apparently at the guard's discretion. That is what made my seeing the full moon each month the very miracle it was.

Although the yard was enclosed by a high fence with razor-wire at the top, I could go to a corner and look out over an empty field. I would turn my back to the main part of the yard, so as to distance myself from the prison environment as much as possible. I saw many a beautiful warm and colorful sunset over those months sitting in that corner facing west. Every sunset remained in my heart long after I went back inside to the cold, and beige metal walls of prison.

One day, I was sitting there looking at this very tiny yellow flower. It could not have been any larger than the size of a dime in diameter. I sat looking at this little flower the entire hour I was outside. Its perfect splendor was a delight that I likened to my Lord— His magnificence was a revelation that I had not known before my prison adventure.

Religious mindset had not painted a pretty picture of Him. It had put Him in a box of judgment and cruelty, which made sickness and poverty a normal part of life—all according to His will, and what He wanted to teach His children. This is a much distorted image of our Creator God; this is not the same God I know. His will is that His creations be in good health, and prosperity (wholeness in every area).

> *Beloved, I pray that you may prosper in all things and be in health, just as your soul prospers. (3 John 1:2)*

As I stared at this perfect little flower, a feeling of love flooded over me. Our Creator God had made this tiny magnificent flower. Out of His perfection, He created something that would give pleasure to His other creations on this earth. The fact is that our God is love. That is His nature. He could not do, or be, or create anything that was different from that.

> *Every good and every perfect gift is from above, and comes down from the Father of lights, with whom there is no variation or shadow of turning. (James 1:17)*

One day when mail was delivered to the dorm, I received an email from a friend, Jim, who informed me that my release date would be June 21. He told me that 2 female friends, Patsy and Renee, would be picking me up. "Oh, thank you Jesus, this prison adventure is almost over. I'm going home!" This email was dated June 14, so I had one full week to say my farewell.

I gave away the stuff I had purchased from commissary. Thermal tops, t-shirts, and hygiene items are valuable commodities, and much appreciated by those not fortunate to have someone put money on their prison commissary account. These people are on very limited indigent programs (usually started by religious groups), providing only soap, toothpaste, and deodorant. I don't believe all of the units even have these programs.

I was so very blessed by, and grateful to the second man I married, Tris Folger, who kept money on my prison account so that I could always buy what I wanted.

Female inmates are released from Gatesville, Texas, or at least the group leaving Plane State with me was. This is a several hour trip from Plane State. I was not sure when I would be taken off this unit, but I knew it would be before the weekend because June 21 came on a Monday that year (TDCJ only transports on weekdays).

On June 7, potted bushes had appeared outside the education building on a dolly. It had been raining, and so the actual planting did not begin until June 11, but they were entirely in place by June 14. A row of the most beautiful bushes I had ever seen. Each one full of little green leaves of life. I was taken off the unit of Plane State three days later, June 17, to go to Gatesville. That's right, my vision came to pass. Even writing this puts a smile on my face. My Lord God is very good—all of the time.

...the vision is yet for an appointed time...it will surely come...The Lord is good to those whose hope is in Him, to the one who seeks Him. (Habakkuk 2:3) (Lamentations 3:25, NIV)

The day I left Plane State was a sort of bitter-sweet event. I was leaving behind some women who had become dear to me, and I did not know what would become of them. To this day I do not know what happened to most of them. Hopefully, they would allow Lord Jesus to continue work in their lives outside of the prison walls.

The last thing I did, before exiting the dorm, was to hug a crying Melissa goodbye, and to tell her that I would see her again one day, and that we would eat guacamole. We did just that about 20 months later, when she was released.

The amazing thing is that in 2013, Melissa and I started to worship together the second Sunday of each month. We live 50 miles apart, and the place where I worship is 25 miles from my house. Melissa does not drive, and I was not able to pick her up, but...God. God can put together a divine plan, and make it work, even amidst seemingly impossible circumstances.

"For with God nothing will be impossible."
(Luke 1:37)

PART TWO:

OUT OF PRISON, FREEDOM FROM SHACKLES….. GOD'S WAY

…if the Son makes you free, you shall be free

indeed..for the law of the Spirit of life in Christ

Jesus has made me free from the law of sin and

death. (John 8:36,Romans 8:2)

CHAPTER 10

RELEASED FROM PRISON...
JESUS AS FOCUS

*T*he bus ride to Gatesville included an overnight in Huntsville, Texas. I do not know how many of us there were on that bus (50 or 60), but it was extra large. We were not on an average trip (like a tour), requiring such a vehicle. This bus had a guard positioned in front (behind a metal grid), holding a shotgun, and it was full of handcuffed women. As we pulled away from Plane State, and were a few miles down the road, tears streamed down my face. As I looked out through the metal (punctured with tiny holes) covering of the window, there were trees, lots and lots of trees, beautiful trees.

Let me tell you, many, many, things taken for granted each and every day were missed when removed from my life. It is wise to be grateful each day for all of the little things that make our lives comfortable and blessed.

When I was in the AA (Alcoholics Anonymous) program all those years, one of the things you are asked to do is make a daily list of things you are grateful for (gratitude list). When I got home from prison, I found some of my old lists; they all had one thing— my dogs, Diego and Maya. I could not see anything else in my life to appreciate. It amazes me that I was so deep in bondage I could not see the forest for the trees. I had my focus on the negative. The glass was always half empty, and...it was cracked!

I will not go into details about the trip, but it was long and tiring. It was not the most comfortable journey I had ever taken, but it was a trillion times better than the van ride to Plane State months before. This time I was going in the opposite direction.

One night was spent in Huntsville, and 3 nights in Gatesville, Texas. On Monday morning, I was filled with excitement to be leaving prison behind. My friends picked me up outside the gate of the unit where I was released, and as we pulled away, I began to sob with gratitude and relief. It was over, and yes, I was going home.

We went directly to the parole office because I had to report there within twenty-four hours. I would be tied to the parole system for 4 years, 1-1/2 months (the amount of time not served in prison of my 5 yr. sentence). There would be monthly office visits to an officer, as well as home visits (to me) by them. There is also an $18 monthly fee. Ok, one grateful day at a time.

I was to stay with my friend Patsy until I was allowed to go to my own house. Patsy is a special and compassionate God-sent friend, who I met a few years prior to prison. I love this woman, who is definitely at the top of the list as one of my most encouraging and loyal friends during the prison adventure. Through her generous nature, this woman sent me cards, emails, books, magazines, and even a doggie calendar. She also kept communication (by email) with a group of friends she organized, to lend whatever support I might need during the prison experience.

The first parole officer I saw told me I might not be allowed to return to my house for 6 months, and that I might not be permitted to drive for awhile. I did not get upset, I just accepted this as how it might be, but....within 1 week I was granted permission to do both.

A good man obtains favor from the Lord...

(Proverbs 12:2)

Walking closely with Lord Jesus often brings supernatural favor in this very difficult world we live in. I would say that I don't know what I would do without Him, but I do know...I would be in prison.

Parole mandated that I put an alcohol-detecting system (interlock) on my car for the duration of my parole. I had the interlock device installed, and began moving back into my house the second week out of prison. Having to blow and hum into an interlock device to start your car, and then randomly while driving, is not pleasant. It is a monthly expense of $76. Interlocks are awkward and frustrating pieces of equipment that dictate how you can start, and continue

107

driving, your car. Getting into my car, turning the ignition to start it, and driving away is one of those things I took for granted daily.

During my stay at Patsy's house, Holy Spirit talked to me about letting Diego and Maya remain with Tris (second husband). Tris kept them for me (and had grown attached to their being with him), during my 14 months in rehab and prison. Tris had also gone to take care of my dogs while I was in jail after the 8/8/8 arrest. In prison I had a photo of my doggies, and I looked at it daily, anticipating the day I would have them back in my life to love on.

I had gotten Diego (a Bouvier) when he was a furry baby of 12 weeks. How I loved him! I watched him grow daily into a big, and beautiful 5 year old boy. Every day I took him on long walks, and I carried him with me in the car any time I could. He was my constant companion. Ironically, the only nights spent away from my fuzzy baby (during those 5 years) were when I was arrested, and had to stay in jail. My thoughts while in jail were wondering what Diego was feeling when I didn't come home (abandonment, fear, anxiety). I would imagine a human child would feel the same way.

Maya (Red-Healer mix) held such a special place in my heart as the 3 year old girl I rescued from the neighborhood to live with me and Diego. She had heartworms, and I had to take her for treatments. I admired her courage as she recovered from this long and painful ordeal, without complaint. I remember vividly as she went over to Diego's basket full of toys, and claimed one for herself. These dogs had been my life.

Now, I was thinking of Tris over myself, and I knew Diego and Maya should remain with him. This definitely was not the old Susan—it was the unmistakable, and powerful love-work of the living Holy Spirit inside of me...*Love (God's love in us) does not insist on its own way for it is not self-seeking... (1 Corinthians 13:5,* AMP)

The first night spent in my home was one of total quiet. I experienced a complete calmness. TV cable had not been hooked up yet, but I had my Bible to read—this gave me good company. Lying on my own nice mattress, in the quietness of a dark room with no lights on, was another thing that I would not take for granted again.

In prison there is never complete darkness, except within the inmate who hasn't allowed the Lord to work in their life. This darkness manifests in relentless noisy chatter within the prisoner's own mind. I know, because before I met Jesus, my mind was a fast-paced treadmill of unpleasant thoughts.

I insanely kept trying to deal with tormenting thoughts by using alcohol and drugs. "This day has been rough; I'll just drink a little wine." "Wine will calm me; besides, doctors say alcohol is good for the heart." "Everything has gone wrong today; I just want to relax and go to sleep." "This pill will help me stay asleep tonight more than just a couple of hours; besides, a doctor prescribed it for me."

The mind-chatter didn't stop when numbed with alcohol and drugs; it usually got worse. I thought I would go insane, but...I guess I already had. This mind-chatter is equal to, or greater than, the continual outside noises of the world; no peace...ever.

The calm I experienced that first night in my own home would be the "standard" of continual inner peace I would exhibit daily with Christ, as my relationship with Him continued to grow. This is a supernatural and priceless gift that comes from knowing, personally, the living Lord Jesus Christ.

"Peace I leave with you; My [own] peace I now give and bequeath to you. Not as the world gives do I give to you. Do not let your hearts be troubled, neither let them be afraid. [Stop allowing yourselves to be agitated and disturbed; and do not permit yourselves to be fearful and unsettled.] (John 14:27, AMP)

When the Holy Spirit of Jesus took up residence inside my heart, He replaced the unease that had always lived there. His presence of peace within my heart, was such a strong reality that the very atmosphere changed. Chaotic demonic spirits were eradicated from the environment around me.

Even my house exhibited this tangible calm through the Peace living inside me. One day a friend came over, and commented that my home had a completely different feeling than it had before (remember the tormenting spirits that had resided in my home before I went to prison?). I told her "The demons moved out when

Lord Jesus moved in". The truth is...*He* (Jesus) *who is in you* (me) *is greater than he* (devil) *who is in the world. (1John 4:4)*. She didn't comment, but she looked at me like I was crazy. I don't think the influential reality of spiritual demonic activity is perceived as real by a lot of people. I didn't completely understand this myself, until spiritual rebirth (Holy Spirit) began giving me revelation.

Am I saying I never have a restless night, or an unpleasant, negative thought? No. Am I saying nothing ever disturbs me? No, unfortunately, thoughts and emotions can still interfere with my peace, and create conflict. I am saying, my thoughts remain positive, loving, and peaceful when I keep them focused on God's agenda (reflecting the Holy Spirit inside). If there is any disturbance, it is because of what I am thinking about—the problems, and not my God, who is the Answer.

CHAPTER 11

EXPERIENCE DEVELOPS UNMOVABLE TRUST

...we walk by faith, not by sight. (2 Corinthians 5:7)

*A*s the days passed, I knew how important it was to stay focused on the Lord I met in prison. It seemed as if every day presented "ugly stuff" that tried to interfere with my peace in God. I had been introduced to our Lord in a magnificent way that left no doubt of His realness. There was such an instantaneous change in me that I should never have hesitation about the fact that He was working in my life (that He was right inside me), but...I knew situations would come (the devil would make sure of it), trying to make it seem as though He weren't real.

The term, "jailhouse religion", is used when a person has met God in prison, but loses focus of Him upon release. When someone is incarcerated, there is no distraction from the outside world. Away from family/friends, and temporarily relieved from the stress of making money, it is easier to rely on the God they met there.

When released from prison, the world is full of chatter that can draw this same person away from the Lord, "Come on, you made that up in your head about God talking to you. He isn't real!". This talk from the demonic realm can yell at a person to such an extent that their behavior does not reflect that of the Jesus they met in prison; focus on Him can be diverted. I now had a relationship with the living Creator God, and I was determined not to let it get diluted down, or misdirected by any nonsensical babble of circumstances.

I had heard the term "relationship", but never understood what it meant. Personal relationship knows the love of our Father God through the living Lord Jesus Christ. It is simply inviting Jesus to work in our life, then standing back to experience the miracles. It is real, and it is for sure—this relationship between a person and their Maker. God will not desert us like another human might. He will remain faithful, bringing us through all ugly things of the world. Peace remains as long as I remember this.

In a relationship, God interacts with us in a very personal way, leaving no doubt that it is Him who is working for goodness in our life. I have written only a few of the supernatural things He did while I was in prison. Truth be known, I witnessed God working many more miracles.

I now had a new beginning, to make the rest of my life here on this earth count for eternal things. In those first few weeks after prison release, I really began concentrating on how I might make a difference for the kingdom of the God I now knew. What did He want me to do? How could He use my life to make some difference in this world?

There was certain uniqueness about my life the Lord could work with that wouldn't apply to someone else. It is probably like that with each person. Choices made in the past put us into the present position we hold on earth.

My own life was quite "unconventional" because of the life-style I had previously chosen. Here I was middle-aged, educated but without a career, unmarried, no kids, no insurance plans, no investments, very little money, and...now I had spent time in prison for a second felony conviction. These conditions make for a rather distinctive existence in this twenty-first century.

I knew the living God could take these qualities of my life and make them work for His Kingdom purposes. There would be no distractions from family, or job demands, as I followed His lead in pursuit of my destiny. I would have to rely totally on Him concerning all health, and financial, matters as I pursued His calling.

Wasn't He the same amazing God that had worked supernaturally in my life, gotten me out of prison early, and removed my addiction from alcohol/drugs?...yes! God had proven His faithfulness to me, that...yes, He is personally involved in my life. Would I trust Him? Yes, Yes, Yes!

I was acutely aware that rough times were coming when problems (health, financial, relationship) would try to drown out the reality of God in my life. I didn't look forward to these things, and would not enjoy dealing with them. I knew I would have to stand firm in my confidence of the Lord I met in prison, and walk through whatever life threw at me, knowing....**I belong to Jesus**. I knew my God would remain true in His promises to handle my individual needs because of this fact, but...how was I going to remain absolutely unmovable in that truth?

As I went through the following months, I would often reflect upon His past faithfulness to me (and to other inmates in which I had been a witness). I would read the journal I kept in prison, where I wrote about how this amazing God had worked in our lives. This kept me encouraged in my belief that God was aware of my present needs, and of His on-going willingness to work out whatever the devil put in my way for harm and deceit.

Our Creator reveals Himself, and will be personal to anyone who sincerely asks Him. Will He do that for you? Yes, of course He will.

Reading in my journal reminded me of how He worked miracles in the lives of several inmates who had humbled themselves, and reached out to Him for help. Two situations really stood out. God reached down, and touched these women in their area of need.

Risa and Evette were from different Texas "mafia" families. Each of them was in prison because of some sort of family involvement with the authorities. Their bunks were in close proximity, and so they had to "tolerate" each other, but there was some obvious animosity between them.

I watched as these "rivals" eventually became believers in Jesus. He began working in their lives, and started teaching them to focus on their similarities (both mothers of young children), instead of on the antagonistic differences that separated them into "mafia" families. I don't know exactly how Jesus talked to each of them, but I do know that after they met Him, there was a recognizable change. I was a witness many times as Risa and Evette laughed, hugged, and prayed after they shared photos and stories about their young children.

This change not only affected these two women; the entire dorm noticed the obvious transformation that had occurred.

The woman Deano, who had spoken to my bunkmate Solma, came to me one day and told me about her life. She had been in prison many times, and had always gone by the masculine name of Deano. She told me she was tired of playing a part in life that did not fit. She shared with me that the masculine role she had been projecting didn't feel right.

Deano told me she had been seeking the Lord's help. He started teaching her about the true identity of His divine intention for a woman. Jesus showed her that He did not intend for her to be a male, but to be the female she was created to be. What a special moment it was when she told me her real name, Leanne. Shortly thereafter, Leanne was acknowledged throughout the dorm by this feminine name, previously unknown.

Having witnessed this amazing grace of God's work in my own life, and in lives of others, would give me the bold confidence needed to forge onward amidst any "trying" circumstances that would inevitably come. I would discover that complete, unshakeable trust is a growth process which develops over time. My faith would be strengthened by remembrance of those experiential occurrences the Lord had brought me through.

As the weeks passed outside prison, I stayed close to my Lord by reading the Word, and constant prayer. I truly wanted to use my faith to let Him work in every area of my daily life. I wanted Him to be the director leading me into the destiny He has planned.

Holy Spirit's leading would turn out to always be done in a dynamic way. There will be nothing static about life with the Lord if Holy Spirit is truly directing; there will be change. He wanted to take me (to take each of His children) on the ultimate journey of discovery, and this involves constant adaption.

Our living God's plan has always been to take care of His children, to supply everything needed by them—physical, emotional, and spiritual. Part of my growth would be allowing this truth to dominate my life, today, in the twenty-first century (I share a little of how I put this belief to action in chapters 21 and 22). It would turn out that my faith would be strengthened, and my trust would be born out of day to day experience with Him.

Trusting in our living God is contrary to the world's belief of doing things yourself. It was truly uncomfortable as I learned to let go, and let God. I would find it difficult to let go of trying to meet my own needs, and relax into a complete surrender of His guidance. The world had bombarded me with the lie that I had to take care of myself by using its various systems. Going against this world system, with the belief that God would meet my every need, defied everything I had grown up being accustomed to (going, first, to places on earth where those things are dealt with...doctors/banks, etc.).

We live in a sense-driven world that says if you can't see it, touch it, smell it, taste it, or feel it then it must not be real, but...my faith knows the Lord of the universe is my Father God, and that He is taking care of me. The world of unbelief cannot spiritually trust in our Creator God, but......He is real, He is alive, and He is faithful. I would go to Him first with all upcoming issues.

I persevered in the Truth of what His Word says, and kept moving forward, knowing my experiential growth would continue to ensure a greater strength of faith. I wanted to witness His supernatural power working in my life to orchestrate situations that I wouldn't have imagined on my own.

God is working in His creation's lives every single day, but His work is not seen, or appreciated, unless our eye is totally focused on Him. I wanted to pay close attention to His ways, and be able to recognize His actions in our personal relationship. I knew my faith would continue to open up avenues for Him to perform everyday miracles needed by this world, and....that is what I was depending on.

CHAPTER 12

WOUNDS ARE HURTFUL; CHRIST IS HEALING

*L*ife outside of prison took a bit of adjustment. Things, and people, appeared different to me than before I was incarcerated. Taking prescription narcotic drugs had not only landed me a fourth DWI, but completely distorted my perception of reality. What I thought I was seeing all those years had been a deception. My own mind, fueled by these drugs, had created illusions to what was taking place within the people on this earth. I now had a clear mind, and I was seeing through spiritual eyes. I was quite shocked and saddened by all I experienced around me.

I suppose I thought I would see everyone as the "in control" people I had always assumed them to be. My own life had been so messed up, I thought most everyone else had theirs together. This was a very wrong perception of people in the world.

This rampant pain was not new; no doubt it always existed, but I was too absorbed by my own issues to notice (to any degree) the suffering of others. I might have given a nod of compassion to someone, but I didn't have much time to listen. It's not that I didn't care, but..."I had my own problems". I was busy talking about my issues, "me, me, me".

As I looked at people around me, quite often I saw hurt, pain, and insecurity, masked in unattractive pride (just like I had seen in prison). These proud disguises revealed to me a despair of inner pain that could only be removed by our Lord the Healer—Jehovah Rophe'. Our Lord's very nature is to help with any issue. There is no problem He can't handle, and there is no person He won't help. First, though, He has to be asked to assist in the personal problem, and second, He has to be allowed to be the Lord that He is, and take control. It takes both steps to really be free of the confining straps of bondage.

I looked forward to serving my Lord Jesus with other believers. Because He completely changed me inside, and made me a part of the Body of Christ, my passion was to honor Him. I wanted to share what He has done for me. I would have to listen very closely to my Lord, obeying His voice, so that He could use me in day to day situations to minister healing to others. It might be as simple as words of encouragement, or through prayer that people would be affected. At any rate, I wanted to be ready for assistance.

I felt sure my Lord would choose people who had something in common with me; at times, it might be just a personality match. I remembered how in Williamson Co. jail, those women had direct links from my past. I believed He would put some people into my life (again) that had some sort of connection to an aspect of my life, and...He did.

I was not opposed to, or embarrassed by sharing any offensive experience leading me to prison. In the past, I had always kept anything inside I thought might not be acceptable to others. I was a real "people pleaser". I told others what I thought they wanted to hear. Now, because of the love inside me, I wanted to give others the opportunity to open up when they heard how my messed up life was redeemed by our Lord. It is in the sharing of our own falls that others will be lifted up.

People began telling me intimate things about their lives. Because I had shared my story, they felt comfortable baring their own sordid past. I believe they sensed that I really cared and understood as I listened to their stories, and...I did.

Some of these people went to church week after week, while protecting deep and hurtful secrets inside their heart. No, the Christian community is not automatically immune to despicable issues on this earth.

A portion of the confidences shared were quite shocking, and would have been fodder for vicious gossip. I sensed this sharing with me was an attempt to lighten the shame burden that was weighing them down. It was not me who could take away this weight, but I could listen, and share how Jesus had set me free from the bondage of my past. It is only Lord Jesus who can permanently remove all disgrace, and He remains available 24/7 to every person on this earth.

Two women confided in me that they had regularly been abused sexually by close relatives. Another woman's mother had abused her grandson sexually for years, until it was found out, and legal action taken. There was even a woman who had been impregnated by her dad, and had a child by him. I had sensitivity to these women because of the sexual deviance I remembered (in prison's changes class) experiencing as a child.

There were several members of the small congregation I attended that had either been to prison, or had someone close to them currently in prison. Many members had on-going alcohol and/or drug addictions—some of these people were actively working in church ministry. Of course I have a strong bond of affection with anyone in the evil clutches of addiction.

It is very difficult to get people to lower the mask, and reveal the underlying poison to their wounded soul. It takes time, and it is genuine love that begins the process of removal. The reward of seeing a layer of shame/guilt removed from the person (remember me in front of that judge) is well worth the expenditure of patience and love.

I wanted to contribute something to this suffering world. The living Lord God had replaced the dead lies in my heart with a love that was alive and growing—I wanted to share about Him. I would find there would be much training in the academy of Lord Jesus Christ before He could use me in this messed-up world. He had much work to do inside of my head.

My mind had been really messed up by the drugs and alcohol, and also by very wrong ideas put into place by the world's way of doing things. I had decades of wrong thinking to purge out. Not only did I need to get rid of wrong ideology implanted by society, I needed to replace it with the truth of how our Creator Love God desires His creations to live.

Over and over, I would have to remind myself to trust God, as I allowed Him to direct my life. I had to practice patience as I tried not to force things to take place, but just let them happen. I watched in astonishment as the Lord put me together with His other children so we could help each other. I would begin looking forward to the "divine appointments" that would become frequent in my life.

CHAPTER 13

WORLD'S WAY IS FLAWED; GOD'S WAY IS GRACE

$\mathcal{I}$ attended a local Bible study group 2 months out of prison (in August 2010). There were around 12 women in it, and God had already picked out one of them (I hadn't met her yet) to help me at a later date. Because I am unable to see the complete picture of my life that God is, I was unaware that I would need the assistance she would provide. My Lord knew what help I would need soon, and had placed her in my path. Our God knows what we need before we do. *...your Father knows the things you have need of before you ask Him..(Matthew 6:8).*

In October (2010), when my driver's license was to expire, I went to DPS (Department of Public Safety) to get a new one. After my picture was taken, I was told I would receive the laminated copy in 2 weeks. Around 2 weeks went by, and I did receive mail from DPS. I assumed it was my new license, but it was a letter informing that my license had been suspended for 2 years on the day I was sentenced to prison.

Why wasn't this detail disclosed by parole, or when I went to get my picture taken at DPS? The answer is... the world system is full of flaws. In contrast...God's system is full of grace!

My first response was to hire an attorney, and petition the judge for an occupational license. I did see an attorney that week, but did not feel a real peace about it ... *let the peace of God rule in your hearts.... (Colossians 3:15)*.

After visiting the attorney, I felt the Lord wanted me to rely on Him until my license was reissued the end of July the following year. Nine months seemed a very long time to go without the freedom of my own car (I would be confined to my house, and dependent on others to take me places on their time-schedule), but I decided to trust in my Lord. He had not let me down so far, and I did not doubt that He would come through for me this time. He is reliable, and He always will be. It is not in His nature to change. God will remain trustworthy amidst any circumstance because... *Jesus Christ is the same yesterday, today, and forever .(Hebrews 13:8)*.

A few days later, at the next Bible study, I mentioned this predicament. One of the women, Judy E., offered to take me to the grocery store. On the way home from that first trip it was decided she would take me grocery shopping each week on Monday. This soothed me, as it gave me a fixed schedule to rely on. I liked knowing exactly what was going to happen, and in which particular time-frame.

Strange, how we (humans) are more comfortable confining our-selves to a "known box". Something goes differently than expected, and often the immediate reaction is resistance. The average person doesn't like change. I had wanted to control the license situation; it took me by surprise, and I wanted to "fix it" by obtaining an occupa-tional license. It didn't take my Lord by surprise, though. He already had the provision ready for me. All I had to do is trust, and give the care over to Him. I would continue to learn through experience with my Lord; to trust Him with every circumstance as it arrived in my life. Yes, ok, one day at a time.

Judy also volunteered to take me to monthly parole meetings. These excursions were a time for us to share our mutual growing love of our Lord (He was new in her life also), and to learn and grow from each other's experiences with Him. Our friendship deepened those 9 months, as did our relationship with Lord Jesus. Of course our Lord knew we would enjoy each other, and relate to what the other said. That is the way our personal Father God works.

At some point during this time (shortly after returning home), the void of Diego and Maya was replaced with Migo and Fe'. These weren't doggies, but kitties...feral kitties. Their mom had four of them under my house. The mom and two of the kitties disappeared over time, but Migo and Fe' moved into the house and became quickly adjusted to a new lifestyle "off the street".

Our Lord's wisdom is remarkable. He replaces the losses in our lives with gifts that we could not imagine. I think of Diego and Maya every single day (and visit them often), but I fell madly in love with Migo and Fe', who so desperately needed love and care after their mom and litter-mates disappeared. I regularly learn things about my own life as I watch them grow up.

It is interesting how I discovered some things about the power of words (especially their delivery) through my dealings with Migo and Fe'. When one of them would do something unacceptable, like jump onto the kitchen counter, I started out saying in a loud, disapproving voice, "No! Bad kitty!". I noticed a sort of crestfallen look on their faces, as they cowered down to words in that tone. This was not good!

I loved those kitties, and never meant for them to feel dejected. I started saying in a gentle, loving tone, "You're a good kitty. Good kitties don't get on the counter". I began noticing a huge difference in my cats. It seemed as if they tried harder to please me, and they got on the kitchen counter less, and less.

I got to thinking that children would be affected the same way my kitties were. My kitties did not understand words on an intellectual level, but they certainly felt the delivery of them at a heart level.

God often uses His creations (animals, nature) to teach about Divine purpose. The interaction among nature is meant to guide and encourage humans in our daily living.

God's intention for man and woman can be observed by noting family loyalty among the animal kingdom. I marvel at how the birds, male and female, mate for life.

Divine intention can be learned from the principle of sowing and reaping. Whatever is planted in soil will produce exactly that. If corn is planted, corn is grown. The same thing applies to humans. Our heart is the soil, and it produces whatever is put into it. Our eyes and ears are the holes in which the seeds are planted. What we put into them will produce precisely this harvest, in our heart (love and gratitude, or hate and negativity).

Things of God are always right to plant into our eyes and ears. There is much toxic garbage (continual toxic noise and busy-ness) used by the world today to defeat, but everything given by our Creator (love and peace) is perfect and positive food to nourish our soul.

The hill country where I live is very pretty, and I have always enjoyed the quiet beauty offered by the different types of trees thickly enthroned on the rolling hills. That first fall out of prison (2010), it was as if I were seeing them for the very first time in their entire colorful splendor. I had lived in this area for 26 years, and had never noticed their beauty to this extent. I had previously glanced at, but not focused on their beauty. As I was being driven around by friends, I kept asking if the trees weren't more beautiful that year. Everyone kept answering, "No, Susan, the trees always look like this". Connection to my Creator God had given me a deeper appreciation for His other creations—a harmony of life.

CHAPTER 14

MY TEXTBOOK FOR LIFE, THE BIBLE

*T*he change that had occurred within me (spiritual rebirth) was definitely being reflected through my choices. I found I was not interested in any television programs, or anything else, that was not teaching me more about living in God's kingdom. If there wasn't something that would enrich the truth I had already obtained, I was not going to waste my time.

It was odd to be uninterested in "worldly things". I had always been very up-to-date, and enthusiastic, about cultural and social issues. I had been in complete agreement with very liberal views on how this world should be run, based on individual wishes and pref-erences—giving no regard to our Creator God's desires. I would have been proud to tell you I was very open, and liberal-minded. I was educated, and sensitive to other's ideas (not God's ideas)—this made me very "politically correct" about all societal issues.

The thing is, I was changing right before my very own eyes. An effortless change had been occurring through a renewal of my mind, during my study of the Word of God. This change began in prison where I was pretty much removed from the influence of another's viewpoint.

Incarcerated, I had not been prejudiced by any type of religious thinking or doctrine about God's desire on how things should be run. I had not found out God's will from another Christian, or from any particular church denomination. My knowledge of God's will began when I started reading the Bible in the "dog pound". My information came from God's own mouth.

Out of prison, I read books other than the Bible, but they were all written by people who had "life" experience with our Lord. I read books by Spirit-filled men and women like E.W.Kenyon, Smith Wigglesworth, David Wilkerson, Kenneth E. Hagin, Oral Roberts, Billye Brim, Ken and Gloria Copeland, Derek Prince, Andrew Wommack and many others. Their different stories about relationship with Lord Jesus encouraged and enlightened my walk with Him.

I was drawn to read inspirational stories, written by those who experienced the supernatural power of God in their own life. People can limit God's work in their lives by focusing on the problems of this world (this creates an atmosphere of fear, and unbelief). **In the spiritual realm, fear and unbelief restrict the flow of the Divine supernatural.** A person not experiencing supernatural goodness in their life is most likely focusing on the natural world, instead of the supernatural God.

One should be aware that "supernatural" things originate from the demonic realm, as well as from the divine realm of God. Any "supernatural" happening not lining up with the Word of God (Bible) should be discarded immediately. Things that do not agree with divine principles are not from God. Events (situations and circumstances) that do not correlate with our Lord's intended will for our good are demonically induced. One crucial reason it is so important to study God's Word is to be able to have the discernment to know the difference.

There are very real, and very evil spirits that can make things happen to satisfy a person's sensual desires. Usually, these demonic spirits work to accommodate an individual in an area of vulnerability (I share personal examples in chapter 20). Be on the alert for happenings that might be appealing, but not in your best interest.

There is a lot of junk in the world to get one's focus off of the Lord. Divine spiritual things are eternal, and cannot be compared to the temporal, ridiculous things that are such a focus in today's society. I spent 55 years of my life pursuing transient things that will not play a part in eternity. I was not going to misuse precious time that could be spent making a difference in the destination of souls. I had to really delve in, and saturate with the truth found only in the Bible. Time is very valuable—-it should be used wisely.

...do not look at the things which are seen, but at the things which are not seen. For the things which are seen are temporary, but the things which are not seen are eternal. (2 Corinthians 4:18)

I continued to find out what our Creator God's holy system of design is for His creations, by deeper reading of the Bible. He tells us exactly what He wants—when we take the time to study the entire Bible (Genesis to Revelation). God's ways are really conservative and restrictive in comparison to man's views (especially today in this twenty-first century). Our Creator desires only the very best for His creations; ironically, human nature rebels at this...I certainly did.

Man's attempt to run this world became ludicrous to me. I realized humanistic views on how things should be, will never take precedence over the absolute timeless truth of our Creator God's ways.

Yet they say to God, "Leave us alone! We have no desire to know your ways. Who is the Almighty that we should serve Him? What would we gain by praying to Him?" (Job 21:14-15, NIV)

I learned some fundamentals about our God; His eternal Truth will never change. The truth contained in the Bible about God's will for mankind is revealed by the described life of Lord Jesus Christ as He walked on this earth for thirty-three years (demonstrating the Father's love).

The Bible informs that we have a holy God desiring to be every-one's protective Father, and that the pathway to Him is obtained only through His Son Jesus Christ....*"I am the way, the truth, and the life. No one comes to the Father except through Me."(John 14:6).*

Our Creator God loves all of His creations unconditionally, and wants to save them from harm. He loves sinners, but hates the evil sin that destroys their lives.

The more I read the Bible, the more I wanted to know about our God. I was fascinated by the purity and love of our eternal Creator, which directly contradicts almost everything the misguided world system teaches.

In November 2010, I believed that the Lord was leading me to attend Bible college. "Great, I can absorb even more." Specifically, He was leading me to go to one based in Colorado (Charis Bible College). I heard this clearly in my heart. I had been watching the founder of this college, Andrew Wommack, on television for 4 months, and I really enjoyed his teachings. I was learning a great deal from this man who taught directly from God's Word, and shared about the Lord from personal experiences.

The problem was I lived in Texas, was on parole, and did not have a driver's license at the moment. Within a few days of hearing God tell me to attend, A. Wommack spent 2 consecutive shows devoted to his Bible college. Watching these shows gave me confirmation this was what the Lord desired of me. I found out I would be able to take the first year through correspondence.

Since my license was suspended, I now had the time to spend studying God's Word without interfering distractions that might have come from having freedom to leave the house in my car. In the privacy of my own home, and from live classroom settings shown on DVDs, I would have the opportunity to learn from men and women who taught in the college, and who had long relationships with the Lord.

In a strange sort of way, the immediate time to promote a closer personal relationship with my Lord had been granted compliments of the DPS. After a brief fret over my suspended license, I had relaxed, listened to God, and was willing to let Him lead where He wanted me to go.

I finished this correspondence course early in 2012, and got a certificate of completion. God may never direct me to finish the last 2 years (I don't know), but I was blessed in my obedience to His direction to attend the first year. I gained invaluable knowledge about the kingdom of God, and enjoyed every minute I was taught.

It was wonderful to sit in my comfortable home and do intensive study. Because I couldn't use my car, I had been confined to my house. Sitting in a leather chair with Bible in one hand, and remote control in the other, I had been able to pause, back-up, fast-forward, or watch the DVDs again, while I looked up scripture to make sure I understood with my heart.

Unlike confinement in the "dog pound" (in prison), where I first read the Bible to "pass time in a lousy situation", I used this situation to study the Word of the God, hopefully to make some future differences on this earth.

During this time, I said more than once "The more I learn, the less I know!". This holds just as true today as I write in 2014. What I mean by this is that the Word of God is alive. It is Spirit-breathed, unlike words in a regular book. The Holy Spirit inside me enlightens what is written, and every time I read the Bible, He tells me something different. It is uncanny how often He speaks to me, telling precisely what I need to hear, at exactly the right time.

It is remarkable how allowing God to lead our lives makes things turn out for the best...always.

CHAPTER 15

PUTTING LOVE INTO DAILY PRACTICE

Spiritual growth, through knowledge of our God, is developed by a personal understanding, and dedication, of putting His "love ways" into daily practice.

The living Lord is not an intellectual concept from the pages of the Bible. Lord Jesus Christ is the very real and very alive Word of God, written about on the pages of the Bible. Jesus' love needs to be demonstrated in everyday life.

I was finding out the world is not very fond of my lovely Lord Jesus Christ. The accepted norms of today's society (self, and taking), are in direct conflict to our Creator God's ways (love others, and giving).

Our Lord is a living, personal God who is worthy of the concentrated focus most often given elsewhere. What should be more important than relationship with our Creator, the One who knows us intimately, and desires to help with any problem we have? Attention given to His divine ways will produce miraculous benefits to our lives.

I continually prove existence of the living God through the "darkroom" of my experiences. As these pictures come clearly into focus, they form a lovely portfolio of miracles to share with the world around me. I continue taking mental snapshots of the lovely scenery in my life in order to capture the awesome journey Holy Spirit is taking me on.

I knew the demonstration of God's love would come through further revelation of His Word to my heart, and would get stronger through personal experience as I actively showed this love to others. From a human standpoint, love is not always easy to do. It is very difficult to love at all times, but the Word of God teaches that kind of love. Life presents daily opportunities to develop, and express, the love nature of God.

It is easy to love when the response is reciprocated, but when a loving gesture is ignored, or blatantly rejected, it takes discipline to curtail inappropriate words or actions. Other people's behavior can be hurtful, and offensive, when they are not responding in the manner we think they should. The God kind of love (unconditional) does not pay attention to others' responses, but just keeps reaching out in the powerful force that it is.

Love suffers long and is kind...(1 Corinthians 13:4)

Quite often my old carnal nature (flesh) rebelled against walking in love, and preferred to get offended over something someone said (negative, hateful, critical), or didn't say (positive, loving, encouraging). Sometimes I went superficially through the motions of obeying God's Word, without entirely feeling it in my heart. Love is always the correct spiritual response, even when it feels wrong in the flesh. *Love never fails.....(1 Corinthians 13:8)*.

Love is of God. God's love nature in my life will continue to develop until the practice of it will be no longer necessary, until it manifests naturally in all situations. I am not there yet, but…one day at a time.

The Lord put it on my heart (December 2011) to go to senior nursing home facilities. I did not know how to go about this because I was not familiar with any in my area. Besides, there is a felony conviction on my legal record that would not be impressive to a facility's administration.

I began praying over all of this. Of course God already knew all about it, but I felt compelled to tell Him anyway. I did know if something is truly from God, He will make it happen in accordance with His will.

It wasn't very long (January 2012) until Holy Spirit worked out those details. I was attending a class on spiritual growth, and a couple (man and wife) showed up to speak. This couple "just happened" to talk about going to a particular nursing home. They extended an invitation to those in this class to join them in their weekly visits.

138

This nursing home "just happened" to be located in the area where I live. Because they were already established as volunteers, I gained an easy entrance into this facility. In the beginning I went with them, but eventually I started going on my own.

The day came, about a year later, that a new director at this facility told me they needed a background check. I was told it would be done through the corporate office, which was located in another state. I was honest with this woman concerning my past, about all details of my record. She said it wasn't up to her, and that we would see what happened. It can be unusually frustrating while waiting on the slow world system bureaucracy, but I already knew everything was ok. I didn't know details, but I knew that God wanted me there, and...He would make it happen. About three weeks later, I was approved.

I began going solo each week to share love, hope, and encouragement with people living there. I perceived them to be sort of imprisoned, as they sit inside rooms apart from their homes and families. I had total empathy with them, knowing what it is like to be inside a structured institutionalized facility, and not able to leave.

One thing really standing out to me was the need for somebody to listen as they reminisced about memories from a distant past. I remember how my Granny Lou liked to talk of things that occurred decades before I was born. My new nature has a listening skill, infused with the right combination of love and patience, to encourage them to open up and share stories. People are the same regardless of age; joys and sorrows do not discriminate among age, race, or gender. Each person has an inner longing to be loved, appreciated, and understood.

I did not have to act superficially among these dear seniors as I offered prayer, and thanked God for working in their lives to heal past and present hurts, as well as thanking Him for the current blessings in their life.

Visiting these centers stems from the love born out of my relationship with Christ. The God of the universe asked me to give these seniors some of my time, but I am sure I receive far more blessing out of those visits than I am giving.

CHAPTER 16

PORTFOLIO GROWS AS GOD PLANTS RESTORATION

*E*ven though there were some very impressive mental five by seven photos taken in prison, those that dominated my "spiritual album" were wallet-sized. I knew the days were coming when encounters from my Lord would be so spectacular they would fill one entire page. These were going to be soul-winning photos.

The first opportunity came many months out of prison, when a woman in a despondent state contacted me seeking help. I met Cherry at AA (Alcoholics Anonymous) in 2008. I had not seen, or talked to her since before I went to prison. She had been arrested for a second DWI, and told me the thought kept going through her mind to get my phone number from a mutual friend, and call. Fear dominated her words; she felt overwhelmed and utterly hopeless— recently arrested, just divorced, homeless, and jobless.

I shared with her about my changed life, and asked if she would like to pray to our Lord. I assured her our God knew her plight, and wanted to help. Because of her desperate state, she said yes almost without hesitancy. Right there over the phone, she gave her life to the Lord Jesus Christ.

The Lord began to work quickly, restoring in her a peace, as He put her life back together. Last time I talked with her in 2013, she was weeks short of finishing the probation sentence given for that second DWI. She had also secured a new job in the health care field, a new place to live, a new car, and a new dog.

This had been a process, it did not happen overnight. When God is invited to take over our life, He works in such astonishing ways that it is difficult to describe. All I know is that He makes things happen in a very personal way, to accomplish things that we need.

About one year after I prayed with Cherry, I had the privilege of praying again with someone to secure their eternal destination with God. This time it was at a nursing home with an 87 year old man, Dillard, to accept Jesus as Savior. He was the first person I met when I began visiting that facility, and even though Dillard never objected to prayer, he wasn't prone to talk about God. In fact, he talked about everything but God.

Months after I met Dillard, he began asking me general questions about spiritual things. One day he stopped me in the dining room, and asked me to come by his room. He inquired about specific issues of God; questions that had concerned him for decades.

I answered from my knowledge of how the living God had worked in my life.

Wrong thinking had kept him from asking Jesus to be his Savior. This hesitancy was because Dillard thought he was unworthy, due to past mistakes. Our unworthiness is exactly why we ask Jesus into our life; our Savior replaces our unworthiness with His righteousness. It took some time to convince Dillard we do not come to God on our own merits, but on those of Jesus. Several weeks later, Dillard decided to give his life over to Jesus.

What a wonderful experience it was to pray with Dillard outside in the garden of that facility, and know that he had just made an eternal decision...to be with the living God. We also said a prayer asking for Holy Spirit's power to dominate. The Holy Spirit took up residence, and began working inside of Dillard's heart.

Overall change in a person is a process that begins with spiritual rebirth. It was exciting to observe as visible changes occured in Dillard over the next few weeks. He had a very forceful language, but began to eliminate most of the profanity from his vocabulary. He also began to hunger to know God's Word, and because he has a vision issue, I began to spend a few hours each week sharing my knowledge of scripture with him.

Today (2014) Dillard is still feeding his spirit daily with the Word of God through audio tapes, and weekly Bible studies.

Our time together always ends with a prayer of thanks to our Father, but for a long time I prayed solo. Dillard would not speak a prayer out loud. I remember in the beginning, my own hesitancy of praying out loud. It felt awkward to talk to an unseen person in the presence of someone else. That uncomfortable feeling gets replaced as more and more time is spent with God.

The day came when Dillard added his own words to the prayer I spoke. He even thanked God for me. Today, Dillard has no problem praying thanks to his Father in front of a group of people; I've heard him more than once.

With both Cherry and Dillard, I was able to use my prison experience to tell about our Lord, and what He has done in my life. My whole prison adventure is becoming a very successful avenue for witnessing about our Lord. God takes the worst of situations and makes something beautiful out of them...*to give them beauty for ashes...(Isaiah 61:3).*

In my own life, and in the lives of Cherry and Dillard, the Lord's personal work was obvious. Transformation of our lives began with acknowledgement of our weakness, and surrender to His sovereignty. Restoration of relationship with God comes first, and then He begins the work of repairing other things in our life.

His personal divine touch seems to expand in my own life (branching out in every area) as my trust remains focused on what He is doing (not what I am doing); everyday blessings become visibly apparent.

As I traveled along the journey of everyday freedom, I was grateful for everything. Daily life is a choice of being positive and grateful, or negative and complaining. Every morning when I woke up to the spectacular view of the hill country and lake, it was hard to imagine that I had ever been in prison.

Little everyday things like taking a shower and being able to adjust the water to a temperature and pressure that I desire, not having to wear shoes in the shower, having air conditioning that isn't poured over my head from a cup, being able to eat a piece of fruit or a salad, sitting in a comfortable soft chair to read, sleeping with a pillow under my head, are all things I had taken for granted before prison... now I would savor them all. This is only a very partial list of the many, many small things I appreciate daily.

On a grander scale of things, I am grateful for the renewed connection with my family. When I went to prison I was not even aware I was missing the very family members I had not seen in many, many years. I had convinced myself I didn't need them. The reconnection brought a realization that their presence in my life had indeed been missed.

My sister was the only blood-family member I stayed connected to (with any regularity) over the years. Even though there was still some stress in our relationship from past choices, we always maintained love for each other, and Sylvia came to Texas from Oregon five times when I was going through the legal proceedings. My lovely sister was with me on that day of my sentencing, and she then took care of some personal things in my life that I was unable to handle behind bars.

The Lord is very interested in our relationships. That is what our Creator God desires for us—to love Him, and to love each other.

> *"..you shall love the Lord your God with all your heart, with all your soul, with all your mind, and with all your strength. This is the first commandment. And the second, like it, is this: You shall love your neighbor as yourself. There is no other commandment greater than these."(Mark 12:30-31)*

God loves His creations, and desires to fellowship with them. He wants to be a Heavenly Father to each person. This communion with Him was lost in the Garden of Eden when His first human creations, Adam and Eve, disobeyed, and sinned by acting on the devil's lies. After that day in the Garden, every person is born of a sinful nature. In order to redeem this relationship, God had to come to this earth and be born as the man Jesus.

Jesus is the Son of God who died on a cross (shedding His blood) for our sins, and was resurrected to give eternal life. By accepting Jesus Christ as Savior each person is forgiven, and reborn into God's nature to have eternal life with their lovely Father God.

> *For God so loved the world that He gave His only begotten Son, that whoever believes in Him should not perish but have everlasting life. (John 3:16)*

*Jesus answered, "Most assuredly, I say to you, **unless one is born again, he cannot see the kingdom of God**." (John 3:3)*

God created humans for relationship with Himself, and His Word is very clear He is highly concerned about our having loving earthly relationships with each other. He began putting relationships back together in my life that had been broken for decades.

I reconnected with a Spirit-filled Aunt Maryolyn while I was locked up. Through our letters, I found out there was a large family of cousins I had never met. A few months out of prison, I saw my aunt for the first time in over a decade, even though she lives only a couple hours away. I have celebrated the past holiday seasons at her home, surrounded by a variety of loving family members of all ages.

The opportunity came to attend a two-day Jones family reunion (my dad's side), about a year and a half after prison. This annual gathering is held at a national park in Cleburne Texas, and was attended by family from many different places. The only other family reunion I had attended (for a few hours only) was in 1998. This was the last time I had seen the majority of my family (except my sister) since 1982, at my dad's funeral.

My two uncles, T.W. and Bill, my aunt Maryolyn, my sister Sylvia, and their extended families were all at this reunion. Amazing how the Lord worked in each of us so there was never an awkward moment; it was as if we had seen each other the week before.

What a privilege to hold hands with my family as we gathered together in a big circle to pray blessings over the food we were about to eat. The man leading this prayer, Ray, was married to one of my second cousins. Ray met Jesus in prison just a few years before, and had not only become a member of God's heavenly family, but now was a part of my Jones family. We certainly had a lot to talk about.

I am grateful to be born into a family that believes in Lord Jesus Christ. Of course I did not see it this way before I went to prison. In fact, the reality of their being believers was probably one of the reasons for the estrangement. Since I was walking on the dark side, any Light shining from a person living in morality can be blinding. It seemed easier to totally avoid the Light of God, than to cross over to His path.

"There are those who rebel against the light, who do not know its ways or stay in its paths...they want nothing to do with the light." (Job 24:13,16, NIV)

...God is light and in Him is no darkness at all. (1 John 1:5)

I could never have imagined how lovely it is to live, and walk, in the freshness of life that only Light of the living Lord can produce. It was in darkness that the fungus in my life multiplied into a deadly collection of poisons. The devil works his evil in darkness.

This growth of poisonous lies in my life was so gradual it was barely perceived (deception), but it was steadily multiplying. It was only a matter of time until it began yielding its toxic harvest.

In contrast, Life, through my reborn nature from my God's kingdom of Light and Love, is gradually restoring all good things to me that the devil stole, when I was living in his evil kingdom of darkness and hate. God gives to His children; the devil takes from his children.

I did not know when I was walking in the misery of darkness that there was a Light who desired to shine in me with Love. I had no idea. This is what I hope to convey—there truly is a peaceful and loving Way to live while on this earth, and...He (Jesus) is available to everyone who asks.

CHAPTER 17

FURTHER LOVE-WALK...
BACK TO PRISON

*M*y growth in relationship with the Lord impressed on my heart the need to share what He has done for me, by going back inside the prison system of TDCJ. As I was driven away from the prison unit on June 21, 2010, I would never have imagined I would be back inside a prison unit in less than two years after release, or....ever!

If there was any hesitancy of returning to prison for a visit, it was removed by my desire to honor and obey my Lord. He asked me to share what He gave me...freedom.

Walking with our Lord is not meant to be difficult. Man has complicated God's love nature by stepping in and trying to rear-range the truth and purity of who He is. The things that honor Him (love and obedience) are not new—they are timeless, as He is, they do not change.

...I am the Lord, I do not change...(Malachi 3:6)

Our Creator God is not complex to understand—He is holy, and He is love. Our Creator's holiness transmits purity; He is without sin. Holiness is not just some religious term; it is the essence of God, and could be defined as all goodness and unconditional love.

The Bible teaches what God's heart is like; He desires devoted love and obedience from us. Because our God loves us unconditionally, there is a responsibility (a calling to us) as His children, to share this love among those hurting who might not know Him.

God takes the circumstances of our lives, and makes them into something that can be used in His Kingdom to help others here on this earth. God did not send me to prison. I willfully and disobediently made those choices leading me to prison. God was able to use that very low time in my life to reveal Himself to me, and now He is using my life to spread the good news about His reality. Our Lord always puts loveliness back into the lives of those who will allow Him.

> *...we know that in all things God works for the good of those who love Him, who have been called according to His purpose. (Romans 8:28, NIV)*

My walk and life with our God give me a testimony to share His love with the world. Every day presents opportunities to share about

God with people who are experiencing some of the things I have gone through.

I am not "working" to please the Lord. I am doing what I do because I want to help others. I could never do enough nice things to earn God's love; nobody can. I was redeemed because of His love for me, and since I am spiritually reborn of this love, I have the honor of demonstrating it.

I have taken the opportunity to go into the prison system of TDCJ with a ministry two times during my parole (each time was to a different unit, and I had not been incarcerated in either one). This ministry is one that encourages inmates to tell particulars of their life in a variety of creative ways (reading it in story form or poem, acting it out, singing, etc.). The point is to expose things that had been hidden inside. I had clearly seen in prison that this was a huge issue among inmates…. unrevealed secrets lurking in dark places of the mind and heart.

When lies of the devil are brought into the light, they cease to have power. It is in the darkness of solitude that his lies grow into destructive proportions. Once lies are shared with others, they lose all authority, and instead give encouragement to someone else that has bought into the same form of devastation. There are always others who have been taken captive by similar harmful ways. These people need to hear they are not alone like the devil would like them to think.

As I went through the first locked gate into the prison, and was searched by a guard, I had a complete calmness. Someone on the ministry team later commented on my composure...my peace came entirely from my Lord.

Seeing those women in their white TDCJ outfits on the first visit was quite an emotional experience. I remembered vividly, the humble and helpless feeling of being inside one of those uniforms. Tears rolled down my cheeks as I sat watching them file into the chapel of the unit we were visiting...I had been one of them!

Many of the inmates' enactments confirmed Jesus was working in their life while they are in prison (of course I had already witnessed His work on inmates when I was at Plane State). There was never mention of any other "god" (Buddah, Muhammed, Allah, etc.) in the many stories from these women. It was always the interactive **living** Lord-God, Jesus Christ, who had come to their rescue.

On the second visit, I saw a woman that I had been incarcerated with at another unit. She was participating in the ministry's program. We were able to talk one-on-one for a few minutes. She told me that her young daughter had been given up for adoption; there had been no family members to care for this little five year old girl.

She told me God had spoken to her, with assurance that she would reunite with her daughter one day. I absolutely believe this reunion will come to pass because I know the personal God who can make it take place.

At the end of the program (both visits), I was able to stand up and speak a few words of support to the group of inmates that had participated. I wanted to encourage these women that the Lord is awesomely faithful to restore the lives of those who willingly seek, and obey His ways. He did it for me—He will do it for anybody!

One woman came up to me at the end of the second visit and told me she never learned how to read, but that Holy Spirit of Jesus had taught her how to read the Bible. Yes, Holy Spirit can do that! She told me how it is her desire upon release to share about Jesus, first with her family, and then in ministry. Wow, and...yes, He is alive and interactive.

Our Lord, through the Holy Spirit, works in each of our lives in a very individual and personal way. Although a lot of what He does, and how He works, is unique to each person, there are certain things He teaches that are beneficial and encouraging to all of His children.

In the following chapters of this book I share some of these things, part of my daily life as a child of God. I tell about spiritual truths that affect life right here on planet earth.

- Reading and meditating on God's Word daily for spiritual nourishment.
- Guarding our spoken words continually to line up with God's Word.
- Remembering there is a spiritual realm, and that Christ won the victory.
- Confession of God's Word regardless of circumstances.

- Praise and worship to our God for all He does.

- Continuous communication to our God through prayer.

Some of these principles (confessions of God's Word, spiritual warfare, watching my words) are developing as my lifestyle; learning to protect what is mine, keeping it from the devil's clutches. Other things (reading His Word, prayer, praise) come naturally in my relationship to the Father.

As the child of God honors their Father, He honors them. The Father is honored as the Lord Jesus' work is reverenced in our lives through our daily walk.

CHAPTER **18**

DAILY SPIRITUAL BREAD

...man shall not live by bread alone; but man lives by

every word that proceeds from the mouth of the Lord

(Deuteronomy 8:3)

I knew it was imperative, for success in life, to read and study the Bible daily. Holy Spirit had me write that over and over in my prison journal during the months before I was released. Wanting to stay focused on God's Word was not difficult for me, as it seems to be a passion implanted inside.

Even though another person may not have the desire to study Gods' Word that I do, it is still very important to spend time in daily reading and meditation of scripture. Any amount of time spent each day will give benefit, but....the more diligence you put into studying what the Bible is saying, the more blessing you will see in your life.

It is not so much the quantity read daily, but quality of reading that determines spiritual growth.

We eat food daily to nourish our physical bodies. A shortage of sustenance has a weakening effect, eventually making the body undernourished; it would be hard to function in our daily tasks without food. Daily spiritual food is just as necessary; to keep our spirits strong, healthy, and in fighting form to combat the non-stop spiritual warfare taking place against our souls.

Just about everyone has eaten an apple at some point in their life, but remembering what it looks and tastes like will not feed your body. Neither will your body be nourished by watching someone else eat an apple. It is necessary to eat your own apple to reap the sustenance it has to offer, and the apple eaten three days ago will not sustain you today. The same thing applies to scripture; it must be fed into your own body so that it nurtures every cell, and it must be eaten daily to give complete spiritual benefit.

I have heard the Bible described as "Basic Instructions Before Leaving Earth". God's Covenant Word to us is vital to well-being on this planet. It, undeniably, was written to teach how to live success-fully, while in preparation for our eternal destination.

It is important to remember as we read the Bible...we are no different than the people we are reading about. God used regular people to accomplish His purposes; Abraham, Moses, David, Peter, John, Paul, etc. were just ordinary, imperfect people who communicated with their Creator. In fact, a large portion of the Bible was written by repentant murderers (Moses, David, and Paul).

Our God hasn't changed; He wants to talk to us just like He did with them. One way He communicates with us is through His written Word of personal instruction and promises (the Bible).

Life (not just living) is obtained by obeying the Word that comes from the mouth of the living Creator. It is important to read the Word of God in order to find out what Truth is. Reading the Bible reveals what kind of God we have, and what He desires from His creations. Trusting, and obeying this Truth brings blessings.

Studying scripture daily makes one more than a Bible expert, it makes one an expert in the Author of the Bible. Studying of the Word is necessary in order to know the Author personally. This does not mean being an intellectual scholar. It is an understanding of God's Word, demonstrating it from the heart—not with head knowledge.

Reading the Bible is the way to find out exactly who the Father is, what His will is, and who we are as new creations reborn of the living God. Jesus Christ embodied the nature of the Father perfectly. *... being the brightness of His glory and the express image of His person...(Hebrews 1:3).*

It is imperative to know all about the divine God from whom we can be reborn a new creature. The Bible is to be used as a mirror— children of the living God (reborn of His DNA) can see who they are as they read about their Father. There are depths of treasure that will only be discovered by deep digging. To get at these treasures, it is imperative to spend time staring into this mirror of Truth; a mere glance will not reveal the riches. The Bible reveals our Lord to us, so that He can be revealed through us.

My relationship with the Lord is based on what I have learned by looking into His Word, and it is based on my personal experience with Him. The more that is learned of Him, the more success will be displayed in life.

> *"This Book of the Law shall not depart from your mouth, but you shall meditate in it day and night, that you may observe to do according to all that is written in it. For then you will make your way prosperous, and then you will have good success. (Joshua 1:8)*

This scripture is the Lord talking to Joshua in the Old Testament. All law in the Old Testament (including the Ten Commandments) was given to show that people (by their own merits) could not keep them. The Book of the Law (God's will) would be the entire Bible these days, and the principle of meditating on it still applies. Meditation should be followed by an active demonstration of this Truth in daily life... this will produce success.

I have listened to people say there is no reason to read the Old Testament because the law does not apply today. Anyone talking like this does not really understand what it signifies. Actually, the parts of the Old Testament giving those specific laws make clear the deep love of our Creator. It demonstrates how He always wanted to take care of His creations, making sure they are protected from sin, and provided with blessing.

The Old Testament is the recording of our Creator's blueprint of life for all individuals and nations on this earth...yes, even for today in 2014+. The very essence of God is purity of goodness. God desires this purity for His creations, but it is contaminated by sin. Our God will not tolerate sin forever. Because sin destroys, it will not be allowed into the eternal kingdom. He provided a way for us to get around the sin problem while on this earth, and as an entrance into eternity with Him; belief in Jesus' blood to wash it clean.

The Old Testament is a foretelling of Jesus' coming to earth to fulfill required laws. Animal blood sacrifice rituals had to be performed daily to obtain God's forgiveness. Jesus shed His own sinless blood to provide the perfect sacrifice for God's forgiveness of all our sins...forever.

The Church (Body of Christ) is under grace. Grace is revealed in the New Testament through the person Lord Jesus Christ. Jesus fulfilled the spiritually pure and perfect law that man would never be able to keep....this is why we need a savior.

> *"Do not think that I came to destroy the Law or the Prophets. I did not come to destroy but to fulfill".*
> *(Matthew 5:17)*

Being reborn into God's nature puts Jesus on the throne of the heart, where He rules in righteousness (replacing the sin nature). A child of God does the right things because it is in their heart to do so...*I will put My law in their minds and write it on their hearts...(Jeremiah 31:33).*

The entire Bible describes the love heart of our God. It is really very supernatural how this amazing Book ties together perfectly from Genesis to Revelation. When it is thoroughly studied, and understood, the power of God's Word will begin to truly change daily life through heart revelation; from the inside, out.

> *For whatever things were written before were written for our learning, that we through the patience and comfort of the Scriptures might have hope.*
>
> *(Romans 15:4)*

> *All Scripture is given by inspiration of God, and is profitable for doctrine, for reproof, for correction, for instruction in righteousness, that the man of God may be complete, thoroughly equipped for every good work.(2 Timothy 3:16 -17)*

This supernatural Book, telling of God's desired will, is the only Truth to rely on. Everything in opposition to God's Word is false.

Things happening in the world (even "supernatural") that do not line up with the Bible should be rejected.

The Bible is not a boring book. I have a mental picture of my Granny Lou sitting on a chair in her bedroom reading the Bible. Each time I visited I would wake up in the morning, and enter her room to that scene. I remember thinking as a teenager, and even into my mid-adulthood (forties), that my "poor" granny did not have an exciting life, and had to resort to reading the Bible for entertainment. I had no idea that this Book would put to shame any other book I have ever read, making them uninteresting and commonplace, by comparison.

I have many translations of the Bible, and I use all of them to cross-reference each other. My granny's Scofield Reference Bible is a treasured study guide that I use daily; the very same Bible I saw her reading. Word studies with Hebrew and Greek dictionaries allow me to see beyond the English translation, and realize the more intended meaning, as originally written. I learned that I did not have to be a Bible scholar, or a theologian, to be able to understand deeper and clearer truths about God. Actually, when intelligence is crowned in reign, Holy Spirit's power is dethroned.

Because Holy Spirit inspired the writings in the Bible, He is the best teacher. When I have questions (all the time), He is faithful to lead me to the answer. I ask Him, specifically, what I want to know. Most times my questions are answered by scripture explaining itself, but sometimes questions are answered when I am led to hear a particular teaching, or to read something in a spiritual book. It is quite amazing how quickly He provides exactly the information I am searching for, so that I understand His intention.

There are many versions available that are written in a way that is easy to understand (using today's language). Before beginning to read a version, it would be wise to get confirmation from other Christians on whether it is a reliable and truthful representation of God's Word. I don't believe every version put out today is in line with the Truth. It is vital for the version to stay close to original scripture intent.

Our God does not want it to be difficult to know Him; He wants our time to be spent growing in intimacy with His ways on a heart level. This relationship should be released from the heart, and reflect to a dying world, the living Jesus. This cannot be accomplished by head knowledge of Him.

It is each individual's choice whether or not they develop relationship with the living God. He has supplied the Word—we can study it, and we can spend time with Him; this is called a relationship. As with any relationship, it takes two in agreement to make it work...*Can two walk together, unless they are agreed?.. (Amos 3:3).*

It was important for me to really know the living God, and His ways, so I could practice being the daughter of love I was reborn to be. Real relationship with Him, and staying aware of His presence in our heart, involves not only knowing His Word, but applying it to everyday life.

As the Holy Spirit guides and teaches me about the ways of the lovely Lord Jesus, I know that God desires for all of His children to walk confidently in the ways of our Lord. This does not happen overnight when there has been a lifetime of walking like society. There is probably a lot of ugly stuff to eliminate before God's love nature becomes dominate in all everyday affairs.

It takes time for God's Truth to replace lies ingrained by the world's ways. There should not be discouragement because this is a daily process.....*we do not become discouraged (utterly spiritless, exhausted, and wearied out through fear). Though our outer man is [progressively] decaying and wasting away, yet our inner self is being [progressively] renewed day after day.. (2 Corinthians 4:16, AMP).*

MEDITATION

Oh, how I love Your law! It is my meditation all the day. (Psalm 119:97)

God's way of meditation is not the eastern way of meditating, where the goal is to empty the mind. The eastern philosophy of removing thoughts from the mind is supposed to give peace. Biblical meditation is to mentally reflect on scriptures, keeping the mind full of God's Truth as a running dialogue in the thoughts, and speaking it out.

The Hebrew word for biblical meditation is hagah. The definition of hagah is to contemplate in the mind, as the words are repeated over and over in a low mutter (picture the image of a cow chewing grass, slowly rolling it around in its mouth).

I find that it is not difficult to meditate. In fact, meditation is done all the time. Worry is meditating on the negative; this is the world's way of daily meditation. This results in a variety of emotional and physical problems. God's meditation is focusing on His Truth. The results are a serenely positive and healthy life.

When my thoughts start veering toward anything negative and unhealthy, I quickly get them back in line with God's Word. I usually have to do this many times each hour, re-adjusting my thoughts promptly back to where they should be focused—Truth.

Meditating on God's Word causes the heart to be full of good things because He is the focused center of the thoughts. To read and meditate on the Word of God is to fill the thoughts with Truth, which filters down to root in the heart. When a heart is full of His Word, it will spill out of the mouth.

When the Truth of God's Word is the focus, there is no room for negative and anxious thoughts. This gives a peace that is priceless. It is the peace sought by the world through a maze of man-contrived methods, (drugs, massages, counseling, etc.). True and lasting inner peace comes only from the Creator God—our Maker.

When a person gives their life to Jesus (to spend eternal life with God), scripture becomes personal. It is Father God's love Word written to the one reading it. Meditating on His personal promises becomes the Truth over circumstances in this world.

All of God's many promises are written for His children, but there may be times when certain ones stand out as being more pertinent. Two of the scriptures I would personalize, meditate on, and speak are Philippians 4:19... *my God shall supply all your need according to His riches in glory by Christ Jesus,* and Isaiah 53:5... *by His stripes we are healed* . I talk about this in chapters 21 and 22.

I thought of these verses, and confessed them over and over amidst circumstances that competed with their very Truth. I knew these scriptures were written for me as a child of the living God, and the devil's lies being displayed through the circumstances were not going to take it (Truth) from me.

I mentally visualized how Jesus, as the Son of God, came to earth and made those verses reality by giving His life for me. The key to complete peace is to meditate on Jesus Christ. Our **living** Lord is the Answer to the problems on this earth—all of them.

> *You will keep him in perfect peace whose mind is stayed on You because he trusts in You. (Isaiah 26:3)*

CHAPTER 19

WORDS ARE POWERFUL

Death and life are in the power of the tongue...
(Proverbs 18: 21)

I never really thought about the words that came out my mouth. I just spoke what I had on my mind...thoughts conveyed into words. Those years leading up to prison were full of negative and toxic words. These words were a reflection of the very "non-life" I was living.

I did not place any real significance to my words, or to the words of other people. Even though I was aware words could wound, I didn't give much consideration to what I said. Quite often I spoke hurtful words on purpose, to demonstrate my disapproval of something, or somebody. I suppose harsh words spoken to me from other people affected me more than those I spoke. Those hurtful words have a long-lasing effect. The hurt injected by words can play a negative part into someone's perception of themselves, influencing their very future. On the other hand, positive words have this same power to influence someone's potential for good things in their life.

I can still hear my second husband, Tris, (decades ago) telling me how much more people liked me when I wasn't drinking. He told me I was nice, and sweet when I wasn't influenced by alcohol, and that people wanted to be around me. I didn't believe this. I thought alcohol made me more entertaining and witty. The thing is, Tris was speaking (in love) truthful and positive words to me. I still remember those words (he does too), and today I cherish them as a reality in my life.

Words are very powerful in how they affect the very atmosphere in which they are spoken. The good thing is, words spoken in love and kindness place a positive, life-giving charge that will counter negative words.

The words of people really stood out to me when I got out of prison. I started paying attention to what I heard around me, and it was often quite unpleasant. People seemed obsessed with talk that mirrored twenty-first century daily news. As the negative reports of the day flooded in, people seemed all too eager to mimic them.

My life was totally changed, and I wanted the words I spoke to reflect that transformation. For the most part, when I got out of prison my words were positive, and spoken out of a heartfelt gratitude for my new life with Lord Jesus.

Yet, there were still some times when I was very aware that words of judgment, criticism, or sarcasm wanted to come out my mouth. I had to really use self-control to not speak those words of negativity, words that did not line up with my new nature.

There was a friend who continually spoke with a lot of discouragement and negativity. Conversation after conversation I listened with patience, and tried to speak calmly with optimistic words. When he was trying to begin a clothing ministry for the homeless, I tried to give him encouragement and confidence in this endeavor. I also expressed gratitude to him numerous times, as I reminded him of the many good things he has done for me over the years.

Time after time, I spoke positively into this man's life (to seemingly unreceptive ears), until...the day came when I got frustrated; I became impatient, and spoke criticism. Emotions dominated my words, and when I spoke what was on my mind, it was not in a loving manner. His own emotions peaked in response, as he took offense to my words; he voiced his disappointment in me, "You are not acting like a Christian". Ouch, he was right...I was not following the example of my Lord, Jesus the Christ.

My words had been spoken recklessly out of a carnal, fleshy nature (human emotional response), and my delivery of them was such that he truly did not hear what I was intending to convey. My words became ineffective because I did not speak them calmly, in love.

This was reinforcing what I had learned through observation of my kitties—reception of words (by someone) is influenced not only by content, but in the way they are released. It is important that my words, and delivery of them, line up with the spiritual love nature I was reborn into. Difficult? At times, yes... it seems to be.

It is a choice, and a discipline, to speak positive words in the midst of a negative-dominated world. The discipline of speaking positive words is developed by what is put into the eyes and ears. There are both positive and negative influences all around us, to steer thinking and reaction choices.

It was very helpful that I did not regularly watch news, or read newspapers (just enough to keep abreast of current affairs). This cut down greatly on temptation to feed into the frenzy of the negative reports put out by the news media (regarding conditions of this world). I was reading the Bible instead, the Truth, and it was all very good and encouraging news. I avoided being around any talk that spoke of negativity.

I would quickly remove myself, or try to change the subject, if words headed in the direction of negativity and gossip. Gossip is ugly, and God does not like it (check out what happened to Moses' sister when she gossiped, Numbers 12:1-15). As much as possible, I surround myself with grateful people who know the Lord, and want to talk of how our God can change the problems of the world. It is not pleasant to hear babble about the problems.

I believe the choice of words spoken will determine the way life develops here on this earth. Words leave a lasting impression. I can remember words spoken in front of me as a child. I believe everyone can call to mind words (both positive and negative) heard when they were young.

Even though my family was dysfunctional, I can remember the words "I love you" being spoken to me often. I had a distorted view of what love meant because of the inconsistency shown, but these words still stood out to me as a potent force. Just think how powerful love is when all actions line up with those words.

Words can be very healing, or they can be very wounding. It is important to speak only encouraging words of blessing—full of life and love. There is a continual battle in trying never to allow any unkind words to depart from my mouth, but I persist in letting my new nature develop.

In my own life I have experienced the good fruits of speaking words of encouragement that build others up, rather than speaking discouraging words that tear down. I have been a witness to speaking positive loving words; these words changed the very environment around me for the good.

There was a personal situation the Lord was working on in my life. Past decisions (both sides) had caused hurt between us. It was a bit challenging because it didn't seem to be moving along with the desired results, or at the pace I would have liked. I loved this person, and wanted healing in our relationship. All phone messages told of the love I have for them, and how I would like to hear from them. I was cautious not to speak criticism that might condemn them for not returning my calls.

For months I kept leaving those loving messages with no response. My flesh wanted to quit; it screamed, "It is no use, give up", "There is no response, they do not care". I persevered with the love I knew was right, until…the day came when there was a loving reply. This opened the door for future conversations, to promote a healing, and unbreakable, connection between us.

The third chapter of the book of James talks about the tongue's ability to use its power to affect the world. It is a small member of our body that can determine the direction of our own life, and others, by the words put out by it. Damaging words are from the devil, and should not be spoken out of a child reborn of our Love God.

> *Out of the same mouth proceed blessing and cursing.*
> *My brethren, these things ought not to be so.*
>
> *(James 3:10)*

As the mind is renewed, and as thoughts get in line with the Truth of the Word of God, it becomes easier to speak His will in every situation. **God's will is always motivated by love**.

It is not always possible to be reading the Bible, but it is always possible to meditate on the Word. When God's ways are reflected on, He becomes the dominate part of the way the individual thinks, and this comes out through words and actions.

> *"...out of the abundance of the heart the mouth speaks. A good man out of the good treasure of his heart brings forth good things, and an evil man out of the evil treasure brings forth evil things."*
>
> *(Matthew 12:34-35)*

The Bible is a book of only good things, written directly from the heart of God. His heart tells of the love He has for His creation. The more time spent in His Word, the fuller the heart will be of God. The objective is that words spoken, and daily actions taken, are a reflection of Him. This is called life.

The Truth of our God has only positive effects, making lives whole, healed and restored. However, it is not uncommon for people to resist, and reject the positive Word of Truth. The negativity perpetuated in this world is very familiar to one's daily experiences. People seem almost comfortable with the negativity that has been ingrained into their soul (mind, will, and emotions), by lies of the devil. The pure Truth of God's Word is so foreign to the soul's experience that it is difficult for some people to accept.

The important thing is to speak words of life into every conversation, whether it is an in-depth conversation about God, or a discussion about the weather. There truly is a choice of whether to heal with words of life and love (God's Blessing Word), or wound with words of death and hate (devil's curse words).

The mind has to be completely renewed by God's Word in order to speak only life words. I am not saying it is always easy, and I am definitely not saying that my new nature dominates my earthly walk yet. I've already shared how I messed up and spoke something I shouldn't have, and… unfortunately I have done this more than once.

At least I have begun the journey of conquering my words, to allow them to line up with my new nature in Christ. There will be major victory when all of my words originate out of God's very own love nature inside me.

WORDS THAT AGREE WITH THE DEVIL

Creator God does not speak fear or doubt; He does not speak sickness and lack…these words are the language of the devil. Our God speaks faith, healing, and prosperity. The vocabulary of a child of God should match their Daddy!

Thoughts are a central place the devil can get in to deceive the perfect will of God, and to influence our words. He cannot read our thoughts, but he can interpret expressions, and observe reactions, to thoughts going through our mind; the devil can hear our words, and see our actions.

Things that are under the curse (anything bad) can be invited in through our own spoken words; these words originate in the mind. It is amazing how, through-out time, negative words of defeat have subtly crept into our everyday language. Most times people speak things that give them defeat, without even realizing it.

There are many common expressions used everyday that are mimicking the devil's language. These words and phrases have crept into our culture in such a subtle way that people do not consider them to be harmful. Common phrases using the word "death" have literally invaded our society—"That scares me to death", "I love her to death", "That tickles me to death.", "That just kills me". What??

Words are used all the time that invite sickness into our lives: "I'm taking a cold", or "I'm getting a headache". These words are literally affirming these sickness symptoms.

A very common expression said when saying goodbye to someone is "Take care!". This is said many times each day, and is spoken with well-meaning. God's Word tells us to cast our care to Him (1 Peter 5:7). Why would I want to take any care? We have a living Creator God who is well able, and desires to take whatever care we are dealing with.

"Susan, aren't you being extreme? Those sayings are harmless." I realize those examples may seem excessive, but I want to emphasize that there is a devil who likes our words to mimic his vocabulary of defeat so he can bring them to fruition in our lives.

Can you imagine Jesus using those phrases? Words are very powerful, and spiritual warfare demands that Truth be spoken at all times to give victory over all symptoms of the curse.

The enemy has subtly ingrained many phrases of defeat into our everyday language. These phrases have been used for so long, they have become commonplace. People give absolutely no thought to their usage. The devil does not make $3 bills. He is a master deceiver; a con-artist running rampant in people's lives because they are not alert to his everyday tactics.

I suppose the negative way people talk seems undamaging because there is no real consciousness of the spiritual realm's influence on daily life.

CHAPTER 20

SPIRITUAL REALITIES

...we do not wrestle against flesh and blood, but against principalities, against powers, against rulers of the darkness of this age, against spiritual hosts of wickedness in the heavenly places. (Ephesians 6:12)

$\mathcal{A}$ngels are real! The devil, and demonic spirits are real! Unbelief and denial do not change this truth. Prior to meeting the living God in prison, I accepted the world as just something that functioned as I saw it. I didn't really believe **there is an entire spiritual world that can't be seen with the natural eye,** and that it affects humans on planet earth every single day.

God has a host of angelic beings that are active as ministering spirits to the heirs of salvation (Hebrews 1:14). This is very good news for the child of God in this 21st century. These very strong creations assist God's children on this earth, as they listen to perform His Word in their lives (Psalms 103:20).

There are a few instances from the past when it seems that I was helped by angelic beings. I broke my femur in 2004 (drinking, and taking pills); I fell from the highest deck of my house onto another deck several feet below (you do not crawl, upstairs, after the largest leg bone is broken). I passed out from the trauma, and when I woke up some time later, I was inside the room where the phone was (this room was on the other side of the house from where I fell). I was able to call EMS. I was fascinated that I was in this room where my only phone was…this miracle saved my life!

Another time, when my car went off the edge of a wet road (I was high on pills), I jerked the wheel, the car spun around 180 degrees, stopped, and ended up facing on-coming traffic in the middle turn-lane of a four lane road. My car was unresponsive for a couple of minutes, and the cars facing me remained at a stand-still (I remember looking at them in awe that they were not moving, and that nobody was even honking) until I was able to start my car, and turn it around to safety.

There were two instances where I had been drinking and taking pills, and fell and hit my head on the tile floor of my home. Both times when I woke up, I was in my bed with a throbbing headache and blurred vision from the gashed head injury. There was blood on the walls, and all over the floor of the room where I fell, but not a trace of blood in the "hall" leading to my bedroom, or in my bedroom (of course there was blood on the sheets). It was as if I had been picked up, and carefully carried; I did not understand at the time how I could have gotten into bed by myself.

These instances occurred before I met the Lord. Why did angelic beings help me? I don't really know; I only know what happened. At the time they occurred, my attention was caught, and I was amazed at the circumstances that kept me safe and alive. I can only surmise that it was because I would one day belong to Jesus, and would have a testimony to tell of His love and faithfulness. I can only guess that His angels were actively working in my life to keep me protected because I would eventually be an heir of salvation, and had kingdom work to do on planet earth before Jesus returns.

The devil is also working, and his evil is active to deceive people into things that will harm them. The devil and his demon spirits work in people's places of vulnerability. Demons are quick to respond in assistance to words and actions that will cause destruction. My focal point of weakness had been in the area of alcohol and drugs.

The first people I met in Costa Rica (at the beach where I lived in the early nineties) became my closest friends. It was this married couple who told me how I could go to a pharmacy in San Jose (the country's capital which was five hours away), and get anti-anxiety pills without a prescription. It was very interesting that this conversation came up; I hadn't mentioned to them the previous usage of drugs in my life.

I was temporarily not drinking (or taking any sort of drug) when I moved to Costa Rica. Even in this "bodily sobriety", I felt an insurmountable inner turmoil. I was totally miserable without using drugs and alcohol (even in this paradise). The demonic spirits knew this by observing me, and put people in my life that could "lend me aid" in my suffering; without doubt, they did not know they were being used.

If the devil hadn't arranged for this couple to tell me, I would have never known about this obscure pharmacy selling pills for the "right amount" (a lot) of U.S. money. After they told me, I was obsessed with the thought of getting those pills. I couldn't wait until I could go to this large city, get a taxi, and go up into the mountains where this pharmacy was located. Coincidence? Hardly!

When I was in jail in 1997, there was a woman (incarcerated with me) that told of a doctor who would prescribe the anti-anxiety medication I had been taking in Costa Rica. After coming back to the U.S. (before being put in jail), I had changed doctors every few months to get those pills. Now, I knew a doctor's name where I could get a steady supply. I thought about this (I had some pills at home, but knew this supply would run out), and already had an appointment made to see him by the time I got out of confinement. Coincidence? Hardly! This doctor prescribed that medication to me until the day I entered rehab in 2009.

After I broke my femur (2004), and the surgeon would not prescribe any more pain pills, I began driving to Houston (around 350 miles round-trip from my house) every two weeks to get them at a pain clinic. I did this for over a year (the insane life of an addict!). I wanted to find a closer supply in Austin because I was tired of the drive. One night (close to midnight) I met a complete stranger in the grocery store who told me about a doctor in Austin who would pre-scribe pain pills. I went home completely ecstatic, and could barely wait until the next day when I would call and make an appointment. Coincidence? Hardly! This was one of two "legal drug dealers" I visited regularly, until the day I entered rehab in 2009.

Amazing how the devil put situations in my life that would attract me, and...yes, I took the bait. He knew of my desire for drugs by observation of me, and listening to my words. The devil and his demon spirits were very glad to accommodate in this way of destruction. The devil is eager to render "help"; to lead in areas that are not in our best interests. After those people were used to tell me where to get drugs, my thoughts were obsessed until I made it happen. Often what we desire, will become our downfall. The dev-il's evil direction is available to anyone who will follow.

Of course, I did not realize there was a demonic spiritual force working against me at the time it was happening (it would be many years before my spiritual eyes would be opened to this fact; Holy Spirit would remind me of these experiences). At the time, I thought the meeting of all those people was a wonderful coincidence. In reality, these incidents were very destructive opportunities that led to a way of securing harmful drugs. Unfortunately, I willingly followed each time. My pursuit led to a deeper bondage, and more severe consequences.

What is seen by the human eye in the natural realm is not the reality of what is really going on. There is a spiritual realm that is only discerned with spiritual eyes. The day to day ugliness experienced by people as they watch the world on local news, or even deal with their own personal problems, has an underlying truth known as spiritual warfare. The good news, for believers in Jesus, is…the war has been won.

> *"Don't be afraid!" Elisha told him "For our army is bigger that theirs!" Then Elisha prayed, "Lord, open his eyes and let him see!" and the Lord opened the young man's eyes so that he could see horses of fire and chariots of fire everywhere upon the mountain! (2 Kings 6:16-17,* The Book)

This very real warfare between good and evil exists in an atmospheric realm not perceived, except by spiritual discernment. Any true believer has the victory over evil. It was won by Lord Jesus Christ through the cross and resurrection; however, there has to be the belief that He has defeated the devil, and made His Church (Body of Christ) victorious, before the manifestation can be fully observed.

...in all these things we are more than conquerors through Him who loved us. (Romans 8:37)

Amazingly, many in His Church do not truly believe this. Head knowledge alone will not produce results. A common belief is that there is only spiritual victory for eternal life. Praise God, there is victory for eternal life, but Lord Jesus paid the price of our redemption by sacrificing His life to give His believers even more.

Some Christians are waiting to go to heaven so they can have the perfect life. Life on this sin-infected earth will never be perfect, until... the Lord returns. It is difficult for people to believe Lord Jesus' victory over the devil in this earthly realm because there is so much evil in this world—sickness and disease, poverty, relationship issues, drug and alcohol problems, rampant crime etc..

Lord Jesus said there would be tribulations that His Church (true believers of Jesus) would go through. He never said that life on earth would be without issues. There are visible manifestations of evil on this earth, and we have to deal with them. I believe that our God overcame these things, and that by taking the authority we have in Him, things can go much smoother than if we just sit around, and accept these evils.

Lord Jesus spoke these words hours before His crucifixion, and I believe that they have a literal, as well as a spiritual, meaning:

> ..."*These things I have spoken to you that in Me you*
> *may have peace. In the world you will have tribu-*
> *lation; but be of good cheer, I have overcome the*
> *world." (John 16:33)*

The devil is still loose for now, and until Lord Jesus returns to reign in total righteousness forever, evil things will be on the increase, but.....I believe that His Church Body has authority over these things on earth today. Lord Jesus Christ is the Head of the Body of Christ (believers).

> *And Jesus came and spoke..."All authority has been*
> *given to Me in heaven and on earth..." And he put*
> *all things under His feet, and gave Him to be head*
> *over all things to the church which is His body...*
> *(Matthew 28:18) (Ephesians 1:22-23)*

Authority over evil is taken by speaking the Word of God's will (Truth from the Bible) into the situation. This is not taught in the average local church, but the Holy Spirit started teaching me about some of this early on in prison. I was not misguided by, or tolerant of, any religious complacency trying to explain the present evil on earth as something to be tolerated until heaven is attained. To attribute these evils as things that can only be dealt with when Lord

Jesus returns, and the Church (Body of Christ) is in heaven, takes the responsibility off believers on this earth today.

I began practicing the spiritual warfare in prison. Two powerful offensive weapons in this warfare are speaking the Word of God as a sword, and continual praise to our God.

> *...take the helmet of salvation, and the sword of the Spirit, which is the word of God...(Ephesians 6:17)*

> *Let the high praises of God be in their mouth, and a two-edged sword in their hand...(Psalm 149:6)*

In prison, I began to make confessions of faith using the Word, and I began to consistently praise my Lord for who He is. These two weapons are to be used in an aggressive tactic to make the devil flee. The devil does not want to be around anyone who believes, and who is submitting in obedience to the Truth of God's Word. Our enemy cannot stand to be around believers as they praise the very One who is the Living Word—Lord Jesus Christ.

> *...submit to God. Resist the devil and he will flee from you. (James 4:7)*

This verse puts the responsibility on the believer; it does not say we should ask God to make the devil leave us alone. The Bible tells us to vigorously submit to God (His Truth, His Word, His Way), and to actively resist the devil (his lies, his deceptions, his evil). The devil will run from the spoken Word of Truth.

The whole armor of God is described by the Apostle Paul in Ephesians 6:10-18. The center of this armor is the belt of Truth—it keeps the armor in place.

I did not understand all of this in prison (still don't have a complete grasp of spiritual things), but I believed enough to begin taking my authority, and to practice fighting off the enemy with Truth. The devil had controlled my life for four decades. I knew the rest of my life on earth would be taking the victory over the devil that my Lord Jesus died to give me.

About a year after prison I went to a friend's baby shower. It was held at a winery. There were around twenty-five attendees. We were standing around talking in groups when a waitress came into the room. She held a silver tray of wine in pretty glasses (my previous drink of choice). This waitress whisked past all the women (none had been given drinks yet), crossed the room, came directly to me, and said "Would you like a glass of wine?". Unbelievable, but real. I mentally thanked my Lord that He had removed any desire for alcohol, and said "No, thank you, I don't drink". Coincidence? Hardly!

Because my spiritual eyes were open, I recognized this enticement as coming from the demonic realm of ruin. I quickly declined the devil's invitation to attend a destruction party where I would have been the guest of honor. The powerful thing is, I gave no thought to taking a drink; I was not even slightly tempted to accept a glass of wine.

I rebuked the devil quite a lot in the beginning, but I found that if I was speaking the Word of God, and giving praise to Him, the devil did not like to be around. The devil cannot tolerate being in the presence of God. **Light dispels darkness**. The focus should always be on our Lord Jesus Christ, the Victor—never on the devil, the loser.

I am not claiming to be the expert at spiritual warfare, I don't have to be. The war has been won by Jesus; I just have to stand, with certainty, in His defeat of the devil. The reality of spiritual warfare will go on whether it is fought by the believer, or not.

As time passes, I get a better understanding of this very real activity in daily life, and personally want to be equipped with the stamina to fight evils that many perceive as normal. It is not God's desire for a believer to stand by, and let the forces of evil ransack their lives. The determination to stand in Truth on my faith-walk comes by reading and meditating on the Word. Truth can't be used to fight the war unless it is known.

> *My people are destroyed for lack of knowledge....*
> *faith comes by hearing, and hearing by the word of*
> *God. (Hosea 4:6, Romans 10:17)*

Being deceived by the devil begins in thoughts (which can be prompted by real situations, like those people who told me about drugs)—this is where the spiritual warfare takes place. Focus on thoughts can become a point of fixation until they actually become reality; thoughts can magnify God's Truth, or they can spotlight the lies of our enemy.

Thoughts such as "You are sick", "God doesn't care what is going on in your life", "God's Word doesn't work", or any negative thought, contrary to the Word of God, would be lies of our enemy, the devil. The enemy's lies should be cast out of thoughts immediately, before they are allowed to develop into action.

The devil has to sell his lies by deceit, and plenty of people buy into them. The lies have been in action so long, that they seem like the truth to many people. The truth is...Lord Jesus Christ defeated the devil (at the cross) through His blood.

> *Having disarmed principalities and powers, He made a public spectacle of them, triumphing over them...(Colossians 2:15)*

The symptoms of disease, or of any other evil, have to be diligently fought against with the Truth of God's Word. The first step is to believe that there is a spiritual warfare that Lord Jesus Christ has already won. Then the battle has to be fought—the warfare is in the mind. Victory of this warfare is unwavering belief of what our God says, over what the circumstances say.

> *..the weapons of our warfare are not carnal but mighty in God for pulling down strongholds, casting down arguments and every high thing that exalts itself against the knowledge of God, bringing every thought into captivity to the obedience of Christ.*
>
> *(2 Corinthians 10:4-5)*

Most people rush first to the aid of the world for help in any emergency...doctors, counselors, psychiatrists, financial experts. etc.. These appointments are often set up before consulting the living God's Word. The earlier the Truth is maintained and spoken in any situation, the quicker the results manifest. Again, the Truth comes from the Bible, but...it has to be believed, and confessed.

CHAPTER 21

CONFESSION OF HEALING

...He has borne our griefs (sicknesses) *and carried our sorrows* (pains); *yet we esteemed Him stricken, smitten by God, and afflicted, but He was wounded for our transgressions, He was bruised for our iniquities; the chastisement for our peace was upon Him, and by His stripes we are healed. (Isaiah 53:4-5)*

A confession is simply an unwavering declaration of God's Word of Truth. There is no foolishness in confession of God's Word—it is eternal Truth written for us to know. Confession of anything not found in the Bible is only an attempt to make something come true. God's Word is His written will for us (His promises to His children), and when spoken from the heart in total belief, God's Truth will come to pass.

Staying in close relationship with the God who spoke the Word makes His promises attainable. Because I have experienced His faithfulness (time and time again) in a personal way, I am learning to accept in my heart that those good promises He gave in the Bible will eventually manifest in my life, if I don't let go of my faith in who He is...my Creator Father God who loves me unconditionally!

The victory over sickness and disease has been won. Lord Jesus died for us to make us triumphant over them.

> *who Himself bore our sins in His own body on the tree, that we, having died to sins, might live for righteousness—by whose stripes **you were healed**.*
>
> *(1 Peter 2:24)*

I go to war at the first sign of a symptom in my body. The symptoms may be real, but they are a lie. I am healed, and I will not accept a lie from the devil trying to make me think otherwise. I begin to speak Truth to the symptom as I quote the above scripture. The symptom is a lie from the devil—I will not accept it.

It is scriptural to fight the devil with the Word of Truth. That is how Jesus fought him. As the devil tried to deceive Jesus in the wilderness, He answered back by quoting scripture. This is found in Luke 4:1-13. Before quoting the scripture to the devil, Jesus told him "It is written"; this witnessed to the devil that Jesus was quoting the eternal Word of Truth. Truth stands against anything the devil conjures up to lie about. God's Word will always prove Truth over any lie of the devil (if believed, and spoken with persistence).

It is necessary to speak the scripture out loud. Whatever lie the enemy tries to sell a believer can be knocked down in the spiritual realm by a scriptural Truth that counters the lie. This works for physical healing, prosperity, relationship issues, etc.. <u>Find scripture</u> that counters the lie, <u>believe</u> it, <u>speak</u> it out loud, and <u>stand</u> on the Truth of God over the lie of the devil.

> *"For assuredly, I say to you, whoever says to this mountain, 'Be removed and be cast into the sea', and **does not doubt in his heart**, but **believes** that those things he **says** will be done, he **will have** whatever he says". (Mark 11:23)*

The Truth of scripture has to be believed over the lie of the symptom. Effects exist in the spiritual realm before they manifest in the earthly realm, but they will manifest, if believed. The Truth has to be brought out of the spiritual realm into the natural realm. The victory has been won by Lord Jesus Christ in the spiritual realm. Declare the victory in the natural realm. Stand persistently on the eternal Truth of God's Word amidst circumstances that say anything different.

I have had success enough times to know the warfare tactics are real, and that the Truth of God's scripture will manifest, if stood on without wavering. Confession of His Word will not produce the desired results if confessed from head knowledge only, if spoken in unbelief, or if spoken, then negated by being double-minded. Confessions have to come from belief in the heart, and be spoken in total faith of God's Word.

> *...let him **ask in faith**, with **no doubting**, for he who doubts is like a wave of the sea driven and tossed by the wind. For let **not** that man suppose that he will receive anything from the Lord; he is a **double-minded** man, **unstable** in all his ways. (James 1:6-8)*

Confession of God's Word negates if words are spoken afterwards that are in doubt—these would be lies of the devil, deceiving through fear and unbelief. Healing over a headache can't be spoken, and then before the manifestation comes, speaking that two aspirin are needed to get rid of it.

In my own life, I have had positive results from confessions many times. Confessions of God's Word work because it is His Word. His eternal Word of Truth stands over any other words, whether from another person, the enemy (devil), or your own words. However, speaking words contrary to His Word of Truth can negate the confession of the written Word of God. Confession of healing followed by calling a friend to tell them details of the pain you are experiencing, will usually cancel out the healing confession.

There was a pain in my right thigh that became excruciating in prison. I have stated that I first heard of all things of God in prison, and that I was not limited by current day, religious unbelief. I just believed miraculous things of God were possible. I believed in prison that the pain would eventually leave my leg.

Months after release found me limping around so badly that people would notice and comment on it. That made it worse because I knew the pain was a lie, and I was determined to get rid of the symptom. When someone would ask me about it, I would respond by trying to downplay the limping issue, and simply state that my leg was fine. **I was not denying that there was a symptom, but I was emphasizing the Truth**. This may have appeared strange to the person asking, but I was determined not to confess anything but the Truth. Did I care about what people thought, or did I want my healing to manifest?

In my own home, I would confess determinedly that I was healed by the stripes that Lord Jesus took on His body, for me (Isaiah 53:5; 1 Peter 2:24; Matthew 8:17). I would confess this often because my leg was constantly painful. There were days I would limp so badly that I would have to sit down because I thought my leg might collapse under me. I just kept confessing the Truth. I would not allow words contrary to God's Word to come out of my mouth. When the symptoms continued, I persisted even more in confession of God's Word. This went on for well over a year. I used no doctors, no medication, and there was no complaining (I tried to remain focused on the Healer, instead of the pain). Today I walk pain free, and without a limp.

Yes, confession of God's Word does work, if believed, and if spoken.

Several times this past year, symptoms of a headache have become very painful to the extent that I could not even read my Bible, but I stood firm that I was healed by the stripes that Lord Jesus took for me. I may have gone to bed earlier than usual those nights, but I did not take any type of pain medication, and I would awake pain free a few hours later.

I noticed a place on the skin of my right arm while in prison. It was white, small, and scaly—suspect-looking. I did not make confessions about it because it was not painful. It eventually started bothering me because even though there was no pain, it should not have been on my body. Because I had the good results with my leg I began to confess that it was a lie, that I was healed by the stripes that Jesus took for my healing, and that it had no right to be on my body. Just last week it fell off after being on my body for over two years.

Two moles began growing on my chest area at different times. Both grew very quickly into large clumps of cells. With the confession that these moles were symptoms trying to come onto my body, and that I was healed by the stripes that Jesus took for me, they each eventually dried up, and fell off. In both cases the effect of the Truth worked rapidly—I believe it was because I started confessing my healing early on, at the first appearance of the moles.

God's healing does not decipher between minor or major illnesses and diseases. None are too hard for our God! Cancer is no more of a healing problem than a headache. The cure is the same for any evil symptom trying to invade the body...focus on the Answer, Jehovah Rophe, the Lord our Healer.

The thing is that I had spent so much time in the Word, and in awareness of the presence of God, that I absolutely believed what I was saying—it was coming from my heart. My faith got stronger and stronger as the manifestations of healing came more often. Hallelujah!

I do not have any sort of medication in my house, and have not gone to the doctor due to sickness during the four years I've been home from prison. Am I saying a person should not use medicine or doctors? Absolutely not! A person should definitely go to the doctor, and use medicine if they need to. God made medicinal plants, and He made humans (some to be doctors) to minister to the sick to restore bodies to health. God definitely uses these avenues to heal.

I am saying, I believe Jesus Christ took a beating on His body for my sickness, disease, and pain so that...by His stripes I am healed.

CHAPTER 22

CONFESSION OF PROVISION

..Abraham called the name of the place The Lord Will Provide; as it is said to this day, "In the Mount of the Lord it shall be provided." (Genesis 22:14)

onfessing the Word of God has also worked in my finances. The Truth, revealed in the pages of the Bible, will work over any circumstance that tries to say differently. For over a year and a half, I have walked in faith and confession of provision. I have gotten familiar with Jehovah Jireh—the Lord who provides, and... He does! He has been faithful to take care of everything I needed. It is quite amazing how He creatively handles the needs in my life.

There have been times when circumstances screamed defeat, but I knew that my Lord has given the victory to me. I knew that He had already provided for whatever it was that I needed. I kept focused on what the Word of God says, over the circumstances in the natural world. I did not waiver from the Truth of what scripture says about the situation.

Some of these situations were uncomfortable, but I focused on my God as provider—I confessed scripture that related to the issue. I knew He would come through for me; I did not compromise my faith in His Word of Truth.

> *For whatever is born of God overcomes the world. And this is the victory that has overcome the world—our faith. Who is he who overcomes the world, but he who believes that Jesus is the Son of God?*
>
> *(1 John 5:4-5)*

In March of 2012, I realized my bank account was in the negative. This was not a pleasant reality. Everything in the natural was screaming defeat, "You are broke—you even owe the bank money!", "You will starve", "You will be homeless", but,...I knew differently, I know the Lord God personally. As fear tried to creep into my thoughts, I maintained the faithfulness of my Father God. I remembered all the wonderful things He has done in my life, and I knew that He would not let me down now—or ever. I am a blood-bought covenant daughter of the living God. I knew He would provide all my needs, and I knew He was aware of what those needs were.

"...your Father knows the things you have need of before you ask Him." (Matthew 6:8)

We live on this earth, and the world system demands money to function in basic comfort needs like food, water, electricity, transportation, shelter, clothes, etc.. Our God is well able to provide for those things. God, the Creator of all things, has no problem taking care of His own children just as He takes care of the birds and other creations.

"Look at the birds of the air, for they neither sow nor reap not gather into barns; yet your heavenly Father feeds them....why do you worry about clothing? Consider the lilies of the field, how they grow; they neither toil nor spin...if God so clothes the grass of the field, will He not much more clothe you..?"

(Matthew 6:26, 28, 30)

"...do not worry, saying, 'What shall we eat?' or 'What shall we drink?' or 'What shall we wear?...'"

(Matthew 6:31)

The days went by, and the realization that I did not have any money became blatantly apparent as my pantry and refrigerator became very bare. Bills laid unpaid on the counter, and screamed at me that they were past due, "Your payment is late, we will be terminated if you don't pay". I remained focused on what the Word of God says about the Father caring for His creations. Earthly needs for a child of the living God do not take Him by surprise—He is well aware of the twenty-first century needs on this earth. The fact that I know my Creator personally makes His Word real in my own life.

For a long time I didn't tell anyone my predicament—partly out of pride (embarrassment of being out of money), and largely out of the fact that I knew my God had my provision ready for me if I would keep my faith strong in Him. He was definitely using this experience to secure in me the reality that He is my provider, and that He will always be faithful to care for me as a loving Father. I maintained confessions of His Word to demonstrate the complete level of trust I had in His ability to get the provisions to me. These came out of my growing heart belief.

My cable TV was turned off after a couple of months. I did not fret because I knew God would use this time to deepen my knowledge of Him. This time without television was a major spiritual growth period (in His Word), not influenced by anyone but the Holy Spirit. As always, My God worked all things together for good because I love Him and am called according to His purpose (Romans 8:28).

I eventually told 6 people (two of these were pastor friends, and one was a chaplain friend)—these people would be able to observe me on my journey of faith with my Father God. To this day, most people that know me do not have a clue that I was completely without money for almost 2 years. I did not want any fear or unbelief spoken, to contaminate my faith.

I did not allow the circumstances to make me afraid—thus dominating my words or actions. I would not speak words of fear. I did not deny that these circumstances were real, but I focused on the Word of God—the Truth. I only spoke what God would say about my situation—words of faith. I stood fast in the peace that I know my Father God's Word is Truth, and that all riches in my life come from Him.

> ..."*Peace be with you, do not be afraid. Your God and the God of your father has given you treasure in your sacks...*" *(Genesis 43:23)*

That scripture is past tense—"He has already given me"—I believed that, and made it personal by confessing it against current circumstances that said differently. I did not waver when I spoke about what was going on in my life—the bills might be overdue, the food might not be overloading the refrigerator, but.....the provisions were there. I was focusing on the Answer, not the problems.

Still, this was not a pleasurable experience. Although I had grown up in a dysfunctional alcoholic family, I always had financial security. I never lacked anything money could buy. In reality, money had always made my life more physically comfortable, and money had bought me out of many jams—including legal ones. Before I met the living God, I suppose I had relied on money to smooth the way of life; I depended on it being my rescuer. Now, I was learning to put my faith to work, and to rely on my true Source—my Father God—to supply all my needs.

> *..my God shall supply all your need according to His riches in glory by Christ Jesus. (Philippians 4:19)*

Seldom did the living God provide for me in the way my intelligent mind thought He would. He used different people in my life to always get my needs met. Yes, it was rough at times because the circumstances seemed impossible—they screamed at me that my God would let me down. There were times when it seemed that bills with a time-limit would not get paid. Once or twice I had eaten my last bowl of black beans, with no food in the pantry or refrigerator, and someone not knowing my dire situation would show up unannounced and take me to the grocery store.

My Lord God came through, and there has never been a time when I have been without food, electricity, water, phone, a house, or even cat food.

> *"...do not be afraid; I will provide for you and your little ones..." (Genesis 50:21)*

The above verse was spoken by Joseph, but Father God spoke it to me by His Holy Spirit.

The Lord sent people to help me in amazing ways. Some of these people knew me well, and some of these people were just acquaintances. More that one time when the gas gauge of my car was sitting on empty, He sent someone to me with a gift card to buy gasoline. Several times God had people just give me money—this would always be in conjunction with a time-sensitive need to be met, like having my car inspection sticker replaced on the very day it expired, or the post office box rental paid right on the deadline day.

Never once did I go completely without God-made foods. Although there was a time or two when the situation looked bleak, I never went more than a couple of meals without fresh fruits and vegetables; even then I always had some sort of whole food (black beans, or brown rice) to eat.

That year God made some vegetable plants grow in the empty lot (next to my property) where I throw seeds and peels. I have owned this house for fourteen years; this had never happened. This property is clay and rock (very little soil), and the area where these plants grew is in the shade. I marveled as I feasted on tomatoes, a squash, and an onion (yes, one) from my very own "garden"…my God is amazing!!

I began to relax—knowing that my Lord was not going to let me go without food; I had faith in Him and His provision. The majority of this past year I have had a refrigerator full of fresh fruits and vegetables, a pantry of whole grains and beans, and several times fresh fish.

Who satisfies your mouth with good things…

(Psalm 103:5)

I was in a local hardware store a few months after discovering my predicament, and "just happened" to meet a woman while standing in line to get a key made. Within 5 minutes of talking to her, she invited me to her house for a dinner party. This was not a large party, but "just happened" to be a very small intimate dinner of six Spirit-filled men and women. The table was set with linen and china. At this party I met a man (a brother-in Christ) who would eventually play a large part in my life (over the next year) in helping me with food and gas.

God had picked out both the woman and the man to assist me. I had not done anything to make this happen. I just kept focusing on Him, seeking and trusting Him with all my heart, and doing each day, what I believed He wanted me to.

There was a time that I got 5 months behind on the mortgage to my house. I got a letter from a law firm telling me that my house was scheduled for auction on a particular date. Yes, this was very unpleasant, but the Lord had been faithful to me, and I knew He would not let me down. Holy Spirit gave me an unfamiliar verse— not a promise of God that is regularly quoted by the Body of Christ (believers). I claimed it for my own, and I stood in confession of it through-out a situation that looked horrific in the natural world.

> ..."*Your home is secure; your nest is set in the rocks...*" *(Numbers 24:21, NLT)*

I knew that my house and property was secure — I just did not know how. The Lord sent someone to me before the auction took place; all back payments were paid, and my mortgage was rein-stated. This particular person did not even know that the Lord was using him to help me, but.... I did. The Lord is not limited to using His Church Body (believers) for assistance.

> *Many times He delivered them...(Psalm 106:43)*

This situation strengthened and purified my faith for future times. The Lord would continue teaching me to remain secure in the Truth that His provision will always come. My God will be for-ever faithful to His promises (to me, as His daughter) when the devil throws unpleasantness my way. Challenging times would surely come; I would eventually lose that house, but I would not lose my strong faith that knew my God will always provide, and...He did (details for another book?).

There are so many wonderful things the Lord has done for me this past year. He has given me not just my needs, but some "wants" also. It would fill another book to write about all of them.

Truly the Creator God of this beautiful universe is only limited by a person's intelligent mind of unbelief. Faith accomplishes wonderful things for His children. He simply asks for obedience to His ways, and for unwavering faith in His Word.

Our Father God wants us to believe Him for everything in life — His Word is clear on this. I am not saying anyone should sit around watching TV trash, and just expect God to provide like He is some sort of "magic genie". During all the time of "financial lack", I remained persistent in focus of God's Word, as I went out and tried to share the love of our Creator. I continued to do exactly what I believed He was directing me to do fpr His kingdom.

I absolutely believe His provisional promises will take care of all obedient children (believers) who are doing their part in Kingdom work, and who believe God to perform His Word. He is God, our Creator — He is our Father God. He wants us to surrender to His care for us — it is up to each individual; I have chosen to believe Him, to trust in Him, to rely on Him. Our Creator Lord God is always faithful. He proves this over and over and over.

At the beginning of the year 2014, God gave me a new job. Today as I write, I have a care-taking job 5 nights each week. The Lord placed this particular position in my path that would have a very personal appeal to me. I have my days free to write, and to visit the nursing home facilities. The woman I care for lives on acres of beautiful property, with many trees and a creek running through it. She has two wonderful doggies that I adore. Also, this woman "just happens" to be the daughter of a pastor. We watch Christian TV each night, sharing our love of the Lord who put us together, and learning from each others life experiences with Him.

Our Father is good....all the time!

CHAPTER 23

PRAISE AND WORSHIP

From the rising of the sun to its going down the LORD's name is to be praised. (Psalm 113:3)

*P*raise and worship doesn't have to be reserved for a structured twenty minutes on Sunday...why wait? It can be displayed each day from gratitude that our Creator God is working in our individual lives (in a personal relationship), out of His love for us.

If we have asked Jesus to help us, real praise and worship is directing our entire focus in heartfelt thanks to Him. He is the "Living Answer" to every problem on this earth.

Before meeting the Lord Jesus Christ, my praise and worship was to things in this world. I did not think of it as such, but on a day to day basis I was bowing down my life to worship of idols. I was giving attention to everything but my Creator, and as I gave tribute elsewhere, my problems grew (with progression) in proportion to my focus.

Every day I was giving tribute to those pills as I put them into my body—thinking they were my life source. Ugh! I frequently gave admiration to people who are rich and famous, as I ignored that quite often their personal lives reflect failure. I wasted my time focusing on things that are not important (foolish and transient things). I was giving praise and worship to the wrong sources (potential problem areas).

Many things on this earth can become idols: money, fame, power, alcohol/drugs, adult toys (computer, TV, phone, car, boat), jobs, sports, food, dogs and cats, even adoration of other people. These things are not thought of as idols, but.....anything is an idol that is taking first-place in the attention of your life over the focus of our Creator God. God wants us to have nice things to enjoy, but...He should be reverenced as the Giver of those good things on this earth.

There is only One Source worthy of the praises given daily by many people towards things that will not matter in eternity. These things give enjoyment here on earth, but will not be remembered. It is wise to give respect and honor to the Eternal God who is worthy. Praise is an outward expression of an inward love and devotion to Him.

"You shall have no other gods before Me."

(Exodus 20:3)

Our Lord deserves (and honors) worship that comes from the heart—worship meant only for Him. Worship should be all about praising Him, not about filling the ego of those in worship. In the family of God, there are no "rock stars"—we are all equal members in the band. The "stars" in God's family should not try to outshine one another, but instead reflect off each other so as to display one huge inter-connected light of praise to our Creator... *You are all sons of light...(1 Thessalonians 5:5).*

In prison I observed for the first time a few women raising their hands in worship. Why had I never witnessed this in churches I had attended? I found it strange that I had never seen anyone do this, and although it appeared reverential, I could not bring myself to do it. It did not feel normal or comfortable for me. At first, I just observed this way of expressing worship without participating in it. By the end of my prison experience I was at ease occasionally lifting my hands, but this gesture was not completely natural to me...yet.

Today this is my acknowledgement to Jesus that I have surrendered to His Lordship. In raising my hands, I am offering up my life to Him..*Lift up your hands in the sanctuary, and bless the Lord.. (Psalm 134:2).*

Praise is an active form of worship, giving our Lord honor for who He is. It shows gratitude that He is a good God—our Creator God, who exemplifies love, is full of grace, and is rich in mercy. Everything good comes from our God.

*Every good gift and every perfect gift is from above,
and comes down from the Father of lights, with whom
there is no variation or shadow of turning.*

(James 1:17)

Our God responds to the adoration of His people. Praise invites and welcomes the living God into the midst of His very creation.. *You are holy, enthroned in the praises of Israel. (Psalm 22:3).*

There are many ways to praise and worship our Creator God, but the most important thing is that it comes from the heart. Religious forms of rote worship are not accepted by Him as tribute. Relationship is important to Him, not ceremony.

*"...these people draw near with their mouths and
honor Me with their lips, but have removed their
hearts far from Me, and their fear* (reverence) *toward
Me is taught by the commandment of men..."*

(Isaiah 29:13)

Sincere praise to God comes from a heart that is born out of love, and reserved only for Him. Genuine praise desires to honor Him, and should flow naturally out of an awe of our Creator God.

Music stimulates and magnifies praises to our God. The Bible tells us in scripture that God takes pleasure in music, and in a variety of instruments to achieve an atmosphere resounding in glory to our

Lord. It is clear that the Lord delights in joyful praise which abandons reserve.

> *Praise Him with the sound of the trumpet; Praise Him with the lute and harp! Praise Him with timbrel and dance; Praise Him with stringed instruments and flutes! Praise Him with loud cymbals; Praise Him with clashing cymbals! (Psalm 150:3-5)*

After being out of prison for one and a half years, Holy Spirit led me to a new church, for a season. I knew in my heart that praise and worship had a depth of honoring my God I had not witnessed. This particular church used instruments (shofars and tambourines) to accompany music from a CD player, and the attendees danced with colorful scarves to enhance the worship.

I have visited churches where the singing was from traditional hymns (choir leading in the front), and I have attended churches with large praise bands playing creative, contemporary worship music. I presently go to a church that has an awesome group of singers, accompanied by a flute, saxophone, organ, and drums. Whatever worship style a person enjoys is their personal choice.

It is a good idea not to limit what type worship God enjoys. I have heard criticism about particular types of praise to our Lord, seeming to imply a monopoly on which ways to worship. Real praise does not come from a uniform, confining box, but flows from living hearts that beat with love and thankfulness.

Praise isn't restricted to public worship. Alone times with our Lord are perfect for showing Him how much He is honored and loved. When I put praise music on, I turn it up loud, and sing and dance to the One in control—my Lord. Praise can be offered constantly, in thanksgiving, to our God for all He does in our lives each day.

I believe praise highly honors our Lord when it is demonstrated silently in reflective thought, written down in poetic prose, demonstrated noisily and joyfully through dancing and singing, or quietly and reverently voiced in song or word.

The Bible teaches that praise quite often precedes victory to life's battles. When tempted to voice words contrary to God's Word, I remember the many times in the Bible where praise (not complaints, or fear) brought victorious results.

> *...when they began to sing and to praise, the Lord set ambushes against the people..who had come against Judah* (Israel); *and they were defeated.*
>
> *(2 Chronicles 20:22)*

> *...at midnight Paul and Silas were praying and singing hymns to God, and the prisoners were listening to them. Suddenly there was a great earthquake, so that*

*the foundations of the prison were shaken..imme-
diately all the doors were opened and everyone's
chains were loosed. (Acts 16:25-26)*

It is obvious the Lord enjoys praise, and that it always benefits the one giving the praise. When I am going through circumstances that scream defeat, I give praise to the Creator God for telling us the Truth (His Word). I remember His promises in the Bible, and I call to mind all the things He has done in my personal life giving proof to these oaths.

During times of financial insecurity, I remain focused on the eternal security of the Creator's faithfulness. In knowing Him, I know I have the victory over "world circumstances". I am in blood covenant with the Living Father God; I belong to Jesus!

Praise should be motivated by words of faith, joy, and love that speak of the victory over the kingdom of darkness that Lord Jesus Christ won at the cross with His shed blood, and through His resurrection.

Words spoken in fear, sorrow, or hate only give praise to the devil, massaging his wound of defeat. I remember what it was like to walk in the grip of death-like misery; I did that for over four decades. That path is a vicious cycle of pain, giving the devil accolades which allow him to wreak havoc.

Fortunately, I was brought out of the pit of despair, and unleashed from the clutches of the devil. I was personally escorted into the realm of love and blessing. It is a joy to give glory to the Lord Jesus Christ for all of the wonderful things He does in my life.

Wouldn't it be nice to praise Him out of heartfelt thanks because He works personally in your life? Wouldn't you like to give tribute to Him because you are experiencing His blessings being poured over all unpleasant circumstances? Doesn't it make sense to honor the Creator God of Love?

> *Praise God in His sanctuary; Praise Him in His mighty firmament! Praise Him for His mighty acts; Praise Him according to His excellent greatness!*
>
> *(Psalm 150:1-2)*

Chapter 24

PRAYER...CONVERSATION WITH OUR CREATOR

Pray without ceasing (1 Thessalonians 5:17)

Someone in my life (including my Granny Lou, and sister, Sylvia) prayed for me, or else I would not be where I am today with my Lord. This should be very encouraging news to anyone reading this book that is having concerns about the salvation (and earthly walk) of a loved one. Prayers are very powerful! My life bears witness to the fact that prayers are answered. I am eternally grateful for all of the prayers said in my behalf, and now I am able to pray in intercession for others.

Prayer should not only be said for someone, but with those hurting. Prayer is a powerful way to witness to another. When I pray in the presence of someone else, it gives them opportunity to hear me talk with my Daddy God. I truly believe it would have helped me in my youth if my Granny Lou had prayed with me.

I did not grow up in a praying home. The only prayers I remember were spoken at meals on Thanksgiving, and Christmas day. Since prayer was rare among my family (at least out in the open), it was not natural to me. I never thought about prayer, because I never thought about God as being personal; I thought of Him as a remote Creator.

It never occurred to me I could ask His assistance on everyday problems...that He wanted to help me. Even though I experienced praying at church, or received prayer from an individual on occasion, I did not attempt to communicate with the Creator God of this universe on a real and personal level.

The first time I can remember asking for prayer was when I was going through those months of fighting the legal situation. A few times (out of fear), I specifically asked someone to pray for me; I remember feeling a sense of temporary peace when they prayed. Then, later in rehab, I often went into a small chapel, got on my knees, and prayed my own prayers. I was reaching out to the power of a God I didn't know yet. I was in desperation from a panic of an unknown situation (legal outcome), and was seeking His help in a personal way.

"God, help me talk to people and look them in the eye. Help me be comfortable around people, and help people feel at ease around me. I'm miserable! I don't want to be in a bodily prison anymore. I don't want to go to a Texas prison. Please help me! Amen."

The shame and guilt I had carried (for decades of making the wrong choices) had become so prominent that I literally could not look people straight in the eye. I felt miserably uncomfortable around people. This unease reflected right back to me through their gestures; they were not relaxed around me either.

God is always faithful, and now I can look back and see exactly how He answered my sincere, although impersonal, prayers of that very dark time. This book is proof of how He listened, and responded with His love, in a very personal way.

It is important to know that the answer did not come immediately. It did not even come exactly how I hoped it would (I did go to a Texas prison). I was reaching out to God, but I didn't know anything about how spiritual things work in His kingdom (I didn't even know He had a kingdom). Because I was sincere in my cry, He began revealing Himself and His ways. As I obeyed what I heard in my heart, and as I continued to seek daily, God was faithful to respond to my prayers...in His perfect timing.

Prayer is simply talking with God and sharing with Him what is on your heart and mind. There is nothing He is not interested in concerning the lives of His creations. It is just like talking with a close family member or friend, and that is just what He desires to be for us. Conversation with the Father God of creation is a means to insure that each of your desires and expectations (yours and His) are voiced.

There is never an incorrect time to pray. It is always appropriate to approach the Father, in Jesus' name. Our Creator God is the right person to run to with all our concerns. He already knows all that is being prayed about; He already knows the outcomes to the things that plague. There is a peace maintained, as the cares of the world are given to our Creator God.

> *Be anxious for nothing, but in everything by prayer*
> *and supplication, with thanksgiving, let your requests*
> *be made known to God (Philippians 4:6)*

A prayer can be spoken in silence amidst this world of confusion. He provides the firm grounding of peace that will only come from seeking His guidance. The wonderful thing is that prayer can be done anywhere, and anytime. Our Father God always hears sincere, heart-felt prayers that are crying out to Him.

> *The eyes of the LORD are on the righteous, and His*
> *ears are open to their cry. (Psalm 34:15)*

Prayers to God should not only be about asking Him to do something; they should give thanks and praise to Him for all He does for us on a daily basis. I personally place a heavy emphasis on thankfulness to Him. Most times I am just talking to Him about what is going on around me, and thanking Him that I belong to Jesus.

When I am talking to God, I try to keep my thoughts occupied and focused with His presence. Sometimes my thoughts wander to other things; it is frustrating when I let that happen. Giving Him full attention will not leave room for any outside interference during prayer. Magnifying the Lord for the help He is providing is focusing on the Answer, not on the problems.

Prayer is a time to listen for what He is saying to me, His instructions for my life. Remember, it is a conversation—meaning that there is not only talking, but listening. Listening means I have to remain silent at some point, in order to hear what He tells me. It is very important to hear what He says regarding my life, and quite often He speaks very gently.

...LORD...a still small voice (1 Kings 19:12)

Prayer can be silent, or it can be spoken out loud. It is imperative to keep prayers in harmony with the Father's will so they will be answered affirmatively. The will of the Father will always be kept if the Holy Spirit is leading the prayer...*this is the confidence that we have in Him, that it we ask anything according to His will, He hears us. And if we know that He hears us, whatever we ask, we know that we have the petitions that we have asked of Him. (1 John 5:14-15).*

If prayer is about something He has promised in His Word through Christ Jesus, I know the answer is yes...*For all the promises of God in Him are Yes, and in Him Amen, to the glory of God through us. (2 Corinthians 1:20).*

Prayer offered in the name of Jesus has the full weight of His authority behind it. Lord Jesus tells us in scripture that through prayer offered in His name, the Father will be glorified (prayer that is in accordance with the will of God).

> *"...whatever you ask in My name, that I will do that*
> *the Father may be glorified in the Son."(John 14:13)*

The way I start each day is to say good morning to my Father God. Before my feet touch the floor, I have spent time talking to the most important person in my life. I do not have any set amount of time; this is not a religious act.

He is God, the Creator of the universe, and I have a personal relationship with Him—wow! He is my Creator, Daddy God.

It is important for me to seek the Lord's guidance about everything in my life. He sees everything from beginning to end, so He knows the right things for me to do, and the right timing for me to do them. God sees the complete picture in my life concerning current circumstances, and already knows the outcome.

I can only try to figure out the results, through my intellect. My own thoughts about the status of my life have proven to be wrong,

more than once. I do not solely trust in my own thoughts on a matter—I need the guidance of my Eternal Father.

> *Trust in the LORD with all your heart, and lean*
> *not on your own understanding; in all your ways*
> *acknowledge Him, and He shall direct your paths.*
>
> *(Proverbs 3:5-6)*

I am in total gratitude for all the Lord does for me. I thank Him
for His help with things that are currently a problem in my life.
When I am dealing with a concern, it is encouraging to me when I
quote back to Him what He has promised in His Word regarding this
issue. I am putting His Word in my remembrance for whatever it is
that I need help with. I know my Lord will deliver.

> *Put Me in remembrance….. (Isaiah 43:26)*

> *"The Lord said…I am ready to perform My word."*
>
> *(Jeremiah 1:12)*

Even though I am praying from my heart to my Daddy God, I
remain reverent to who He is. He is the Holy Creator of Heaven and
Earth, and everything in it. I ask God to show me what His specific
will for me is that day. I also ask forgiveness for any ways that I have
been out of line with His perfection:

"Amazing Father God, Creator of everything beautiful, thank You for always blessing. Please forgive any thoughts and actions that do not line up with Your will. Thank You for working in the lives of those I love. Lord, show me what You want from me today. I pray to give You honor with my life. I love You! In Jesus' Name, Amen."

I believe powerful prayer comes directly from the heart of the person praying, and that it is spoken in their own words. Keep it real, and keep it simple. It seems that prayers spoken out of religious repetition are impersonal to the point of not being heard by the Father.

> *And when you pray, do not use vain repetitions as the heathen do. For they think that they will be heard for their many word. (Matthew 6:7)*

I want my personal emotions to be secured all day long by a foundation that will withstand whatever the world throws at me. This is accomplished by talking with the all-powerful Creator God who is the only One revealing Truth in my life. Praying keeps me calm and joyful amongst the turmoil of the world. It is important to firmly set my peace (for the day) with prayer first thing in the morning.

> *This is the day the Lord has made; we will rejoice and be glad in it. (Psalm 118:24)*

There are potential hurricanes each day, but by anchoring my day with the strong foundation of the love and Truth of the living God, these blustery annoyances usually pass over without damage. The living Lord will bring me though any storm, giving me the victory in all disturbances. I just have to pray, cast my care, thank Him, and trust.

> *"...When you pass through the waters, I will be with you; and through the rivers, they shall not overflow you. When you walk through the fire you shall not be burned, nor shall the flame scorch you..."*
>
> *(Isaiah 43:2)*

On your knees, head-bowed types of prayer are reverential to our Holy Father God, and should be done often. The majority of my prayers, however, are spoken informally throughout the day from a bowed heart. I am in continual conversation with God all day long talking about issues in my own life, and about what is going on in the world around me.

Prayer is definitely not just for my own interests. There is a dying world full of broken people. These people are hurting, and need help from the living Lord Jesus. This includes personal, as well as social issues; it encompasses local, national, and international concerns. I want this world to experience heaven invading earth, through prayers that line up with His will of righteousness.

Our Lord wants His children to pray for others. There have been times I did not want to pray for someone that had done me wrong, and hurt me. When an intended offense is directed towards me, I need to get out of my pride, and talk to my Father God. I can't know what happened to this person to make them react the way they did, but I can know for sure that they need our Creator God's guidance in their life (we all do). This is where a child of God can influence another person's future through prayer.

> *You will make your prayer to Him, and He will hear you...He will even deliver the one [for whom you intercede] who is not innocent; yes, he will be delivered through the cleanness of your hands.*
>
> *(Job 22:27,30, AMP)*

As we pray for God to work in the lives of people, we are blessed also. There are rewards for thinking of others instead of ourselves. God knows whether we are praying for others out of our love for them, or if we are praying to Him to try and receive something. It is out of heart sincerity, in putting someone else first (before ourselves), that we are blessed beyond imagination.

> *After Job had prayed for his friends the Lord made him prosperous again and gave him twice as much as he had before. (Job 42:10, NIV)*

225

I found out that the living God's will is only good. I learned what His will is from reading His Word from the Bible. He is an awesome God that loves unconditionally, and desires the best for His creations. Today my prayers are focused on gratitude and thanks for all He has already done for the world.

Having prayed in accordance with His will, and thanking Him for it, assures an affirmative answer, but it does not promise immediate manifestation. I try not to get discouraged. I have discovered that, quite often, God's timetable differs from my time schedule. I need to remain patient. It will come to pass!

> *...do not forget this one thing, that with the Lord one day is as a thousand years, and a thousand years as one day. (2 Peter 3:8)*

FINAL THOUGHTS

*I*t has been almost 4 years since I was released from prison (June 21, 2010). During that time, I have spent a lot of time with the Lord. He is my life. I want to learn and absorb everything I can about Him, so that my own life will be permeated by His presence of love and truth.

I continue to learn and grow in Him daily. It seems I have barely scratched the surface of the depths of riches in His Word. I delight as He continues to faithfully give me new revelations about His Kingdom realities...*forgetting what is behind, and straining toward what is ahead, I press on toward the goal to win the prize for which God has called me heavenward in Christ Jesus (Phillippians 3:13-14)..*

I pray that my journey with Him has been inspiring, and that it has put a desire for you to know Lord Jesus Christ as your personal Savior.

I include this prayer (you can say your own words) in the event that you want to invite Him into your life. I can truthfully say that this will be the best decision you will ever make. He will change your life to a degree that you could not have imagined.

SALVATION PRAYER
(TO BE BELIEVED IN YOUR HEART,
AND TO BE PRAYED OUT LOUD)

*H*eavenly Father, I need a savior. I have sinned against You, and I ask for forgiveness. I believe You sent Your Son, Jesus Christ, to earth to pay for my sins, by shedding His blood unto death. I believe His blood covers all my sins—past, present, and future. I believe that He was buried, and that He arose from the grave to give me eternal life with You. I thank You for giving Your Son for me, Father God.

I invite You, Jesus Christ, into my life, and I gratefully receive You as my Lord and Savior today, and forever. Thank You Lord Jesus Christ for Your work on the cross, and Your resurrection into eternal life.

I pray in Jesus' Name…Amen.

HALLELUJAH, AND WELCOME TO THE FAMILY!

PRAYER FOR
IMMERSION OF THE HOLY SPIRIT

*F*ather God of creation, I am reborn of Your nature. I am now Your child, and I want everything you have for me. I desire all Your power to come upon me. I am relinquishing "self" to be immersed into Your ways.

Holy Spirit, welcome! Thank You for saturating my life with the power of God. Thank You for filling my mind with wisdom, and my heart with the love of Christ.

I give praise, honor, and thanks to my Holy God.

In Jesus' Name…Amen

CPSIA information can be obtained at www.ICGtesting.com
Printed in the USA
LVOW05s1423011014

406774LV00010B/121/P